GOOD

The Complete

DOGS

A-to-Z Guide for When

BAD

Your Dog Misbehaves

HABITS

Jeanne Carlson
with Ranny Green

Another idea from becker & mayer!

FIRESIDE BOOKS
Simon & Schuster
New York   London   Toronto   Sydney

Another idea from becker & mayer!

Copyright © 1995 by Jeanne Carlson and Ranny Green

This edition specially printed for Barnes & Noble Books
by Simon & Schuster, Inc.

2006 Barnes & Noble Books

ISBN-13: 978-1-4165-3550-8
ISBN-10:   1-4165-3550-0

Printed and bound in the United States of America

08   MC   9   8   7   6   5   4   3

This book is dedicated to all the dogs who
continue to share their hearts with us
in spite of our strange human ways.

—J.C.

To my parents, Walter and Ruby Green,
both of whom are deceased, for instilling in
me at an early age a deep-rooted compassion and empathy for the animal kingdom.
To my family—wife Mary, daughters Tamara
and Stacy, and son Matthew—for their patience, understanding, and encouragement
throughout this project.

—R.G.

Acknowledgments

I wouldn't have survived the endless writing of this book if my sweet old Doberman, Buddy, hadn't taken it upon himself to remind me, with persistent nudges, looks, and mutterings, that the fire needed wood, that it was time to eat, that he needed his daily run in the woods, or that it was simply time for a good howl together. He made it clear that I shouldn't neglect the dog while writing about responsible dog care!

To my editor, Betsy Radin, and to my copy editors, Toni Rachiele and Donna Ryan, I offer much thanks, for their patient guidance and magic with words. Much appreciation also to Emily Hall, at Becker & Mayer, for her work on the manuscript and her computer and word skills, and to Jessamyn West for entering the typed manuscript into the computer and deciphering my zillions of typos! I am very grateful to Nancy Burnett for taking the photos from which the illustrations were done.

Also great appreciation and thanks to the Monks of New Skete, in Cambridge, New York (Authors of *How to Be Your Dog's Best Friend* and *The Art of Raising a Puppy*), for reviewing the manuscript and for the inclusion of my *"Good Puppy!"* video in their wise, sweet, and wonderful book *The Art of Raising a Puppy*.

Much thanks also to September B. Morn, in Marblemount, Washington, for her years of doggy experience as put forth so humorously and thoroughly in her book *Dogs Love to Please, We Teach Them How*, and in her quarterly magazine, *Fetch the Paper: The Magazine for Folks Whose Dogs Are Like Family*. Her knowledge runs deep.

And last, but definitely not least, many many thanks to my friends, family, neighbors, and littermates, who so patiently encouraged me and put up with my perpetual moans and mutterings about THE BOOK, THE BOOK, THE BOOK!

Contents

Contents

INTRODUCTION:
WELCOME TO
THE WORLD
OF DOGS

D ogs have been our companions, friends, protectors, and
helpers for thousands of years. As dear as they are to us,
our dogs will inevitably develop a few bad habits. When
this happens, it is all too easy for us to forget why we ever made each
other happy in the first place.

It is up to us to help solve our dogs' behavior problems. The dogs
are living in *our* world and by *our* rules, so we need to show them how
man and beast can live together in a peaceable kingdom. It remains
a sad truth that many dogs end up abused, abandoned, in animal
shelters, or euthanized simply because their owners failed to understand how to help their canine companions live happily with them.

To prevent your dog from ending up in the doghouse—or worse,
the dog pound—you need to train him how to be well-mannered.
Remember, he instinctively knows how to live as a dog, but dogs'
rules are not our rules, and therein lies the problem.

It is your job as caregiver to teach your dog how to live in harmony with you. If you don't provide guidance, he will live by his own rules, which will be very different from yours. To teach him effectively, you'll need to know how your dog thinks and why he behaves the way he does. This book will provide you with the insights and tools you'll need to turn your dog's bad habits into good ones so that you and your dog can enjoy mutual friendship, compassion, understanding, and respect.

Like us, dogs are mammals and need to live in family groups or packs. For their physical health, they require exercise, comfortable shelter, good nutrition, grooming, and regular veterinary care. For their emotional health, they need companionship, appreciation, acceptance, understanding, and a free exchange of love and affection.

For peace of mind, dogs must feel comfortable with their human family, know how they fit into the pack hierarchy, and trust that they will be treated fairly. Since many dogs were bred to be helpers, they need to have a purpose. They also need to know that you respect their intelligence and value their friendship.

Dogs have as much to teach us as we have to teach them. Their endless capacity for unconditional love, acceptance, and forgiveness provides us with countless opportunities to respond in kind. Their unpretentious nature, sense of humor, and spontaneity help remind us to stay in the moment and take life less seriously. Their ability to connect with the natural world helps us to experience nature more fully. It's amazing and wonderful indeed that two such different creatures can enjoy each other's company and take such delight in shared experiences.

Good Dogs, Bad Habits is not simply a behavior book; it is also a guide to meeting your dog's needs. You will see that by providing your dog with a quality of life that is warm and loving, you can actually prevent many—in fact, most—behavior problems.

How Dogs Think
and Learn

D ogs are meant to live in packs, or in family groups; to hunt, breed, and raise their young together; and to protect each other. Each pack has a pecking order with the alpha animal—the strongest, both mentally and physically—at the top. The pecking order continues downward, ending with the animal with the least power.

When a dog lives with a human family (even a family of one), that family becomes that dog's pack. This family, too, needs to have a caring and confident pack leader to keep things under control. If there is no pack leader, the dog will attempt to assume leadership himself, since someone has to do it. The lack of a leader can be very confusing for your dog, because he never knows what the limits are. Once your dog knows his place in the pack, he can relax and get on with being a dog. However, if he's on top, you might not feel so relaxed! A dog who feels himself to be the pack leader might growl or bite to keep you in line, creating a dangerous and unpleasant situation. It is essential that you establish yourself as the pack leader.

Training Your Dog

O bedience training is a kind and effective way to establish yourself as the pack leader. The exercises will teach your dog to assume and maintain certain body positions and thus control himself around you, and this will help convince him that *you* are the one in charge. Once your dog recognizes you as the lead dog, he will try to please you, because he needs your approval to stay in the pack, thus ensuring his survival.

As pack leader, it is important for you to treat your dog fairly. Keep in mind the following guidelines:

1. Be positive: Emphasize good behavior rather than poor behavior. Give your dog praise whenever possible.

2. Be observant: Spend time just watching your dog as he goes about being a dog. Learn to understand his body language in all its subtleties. Watch his eyes, ears, facial expressions, the way he carries his tail. This knowledge will enrich your relationship with him and will enable you to correct him while he is still thinking of misbehaving, before he begins to act.

3. Be consistent: You must correct your dog each time he acts out a bad habit if you want him to learn. Inconsistency teaches your dog not to take you seriously. Teach your dog the rules, and don't change them.

4. Be in the moment: Correct your dog only if you catch him in the act of misbehaving, or just as he's about to do so. Dogs learn from immediate results. Two minutes after he has consumed the roast beef off the counter is too late to correct him. A correction after the crime will only create confusion and mistrust.

5. Be sensitive: Keep your commands and corrections as mild as possible—just strong enough to get your message across. As your dog learns, give him opportunities to show you that he can respond to less firm commands. Eventually your communications may become so subtle that others will hardly see your signals. You and your dog will have the secret between you.

6. Be appreciative: If you are sincere in your appreciation of your dog's learning progress, your dog will want to please you more, because he knows you really care and he knows you respect his efforts to try to fit into your world.

7. Be understanding: Try to understand each situation from your dog's perspective. Everything he does—jumping up, digging, barking—is natural to him. The problems arise when canine behavior doesn't fit into your way of life. Take into account your dog's need for exercise, training, companionship, quiet time, play, and love. If you neglect any one of these needs, your dog may misbehave. Before you blame your dog for his bad behavior, check to see that all of his basic needs are being met.

8. Be patient: Don't be discouraged if you don't get results immediately. Before your dog's bad habits will change, you also have to change your own habitual ways of reacting and interacting.

9. Be your dog's best friend: You are the center of your dog's world. It was your choice to bring him into your home, so remember to include him in your life as much as possible. Many bad habits are nothing more than schemes to get your attention. If you remember this, you'll be well on your way to having a best friend in return.

10. Be easy on yourself: Raising a good dog takes work. You may feel anger, frustration, or guilt along the way, but you will also feel joy, satisfaction, peace, and love. Expect to have both positive and negative feelings, and never give up.

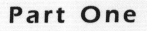

Part One

OBEDIENCE 101

Why Obedience-
Train Your Dog?

Once you begin a structured obedience program with your dog, many bad habits will disappear on their own. Obedience training will give your dog a way to please you. It will also teach your dog to take you seriously. Training will help your dog develop a "conscience"—which your dog will need if he is going to remember not to repeat the crime.

Formal obedience training is also vital for your dog's safety. It gives you and your dog a common vocabulary to work with. Teaching your dog the meaning of various commands *before* a dangerous situation arises may save his life one day. If your dog knows what "come" and "stay" mean, you will be able to control him when it is most necessary.

Obedience training is a form of quality time between you and your dog, and it opens the door to communication between you and him. It also helps to establish you as pack leader. This strengthens his allegiance to you, and a stronger bond develops as a result.

Some dogs have no idea how they fit into their human family, and they are visibly relieved once formal training begins, because they finally have a lead animal (you) to follow! On an exercise as simple as the sit-stay, the eye contact between you and your dog can take on a whole new dimension, as your dog suddenly sees you in a different light.

Dogs of all temperaments and personality types can benefit from structured training. It will help a wild, unfocused dog center his attention, focus his thoughts, and calm down. A dog who is very submissive and timid will gain confidence through obedience training. For a dog who thinks himself higher than his human in the pack hierarchy, obedience training is a kind and safe way to slowly change his mind about his perceived status and begin to view you as the lead dog.

The obedience lessons presented here are sit, sit-stay, heel, down, down-stay, and come. Read each exercise several times and visualize what you'll be doing.

Make the training sessions fun for your dog. Give him lots of encouragement and praise, and vary the command sequences to keep him guessing about what's coming next. Start each lesson by reviewing the commands he knows best. Practice heeling to wake up a lazy dog and to exercise an active dog, changing your pace and direction frequently. Keep his tail wagging! Speak in a whisper sometimes, as though you are sharing a secret together. Other times, be animated. If you are in a bad mood, don't train your dog. Just take him to the park and relax with him.

Each training session should contain three elements: focused learning, play breaks, and calming massage. The play can be as simple as throwing a toy for him to play with, and the massage can be done casually while he is seated by your side. Be sure to end each training session before your dog gets bored and after he has just done a good job following your instructions.

Dogs learn best in short, frequent training sessions. Practice, for example, three times a day for ten minutes each session, for a total of thirty minutes a day. Or hold two sessions a day of twenty minutes each, for a total of forty minutes. The younger the dog, the shorter his attention span will be; a puppy will be happy with two to five minutes of focused learning repeated three to five times a day.

Remember to give your dog the corresponding hand signal every time you give the verbal command. This will help him learn the commands, and eventually he will respond to the hand signals alone. This can be useful in noisy situations or when you need to be silent and subtle about giving commands (such as when your mother-in-law is asleep on the couch!).

Surprise your dog with quickie drills on commands that he knows fairly well—for example: heeling with sits, a sit-stay followed by come, and then a down-stay. The entire sequence can take three minutes and can be done anywhere.

When you are training your dog, it is important for him to respond quickly when you give a command, but don't drill him over and over again to try to perfect something that is good enough already. If your dog chooses to sit casually on one hip while you chat with a friend, that's fine. As long as he is cooperative, pays attention, and is happy to respond to you, don't worry about perfection.

The basic obedience instructions here are not meant to be a substitute for the help of a professional dog trainer. There are other more advanced commands that your dog would benefit from and that you might enjoy teaching. If you are having problems, do some research and find a trainer whose methods you like and respect. A little help goes a long way. If you want to prepare your dog for competition in the obedience ring, you will need to enroll in a specially designed class.

A SPECIAL PROBLEM: AGGRESSION TOWARD PEOPLE

D ogs can become aggressive for many reasons, including lack of early puppy handling, obedience training, and socialization. An abused dog is likely to become aggressive; so is a dog who is teased through a fence, tied up and taunted, or played with too roughly.

Your dog may be perfectly respectful with you and a monster with other people, or he may be dominant with you as well as with others. Dogs who are allowed to dominate their owners will have no qualms about dominating others.

If your dog is aggressive toward you or others, growling, snapping or biting for any reason at any time, it is imperative that you *seek professional help*. If your dog hasn't bitten yet, but is growling or snapping, take this warning seriously and get help before someone gets bitten.

Aggression toward you, the owner, is a particularly upsetting problem and a difficult one to correct. If your dog literally bites the hand that feeds him, you must seek the help of a professional dog trainer.

Aggressiveness usually begins early in a dog's life. When you bring your new pup home, that pup will view you either as a mama dog who sets the rules or as a littermate who can be pushed around. If he regards you as a littermate, he may growl at you when you try to take his food away or if you disturb him when he is resting. If you try to stop him from nipping at you, he will sass back.

If you do not get control over your pup at this tender age and teach him that you are the top dog, your pup will grow up thinking he's pretty tough. When your little pup growls over his food bowl, you might find his behavior cute. You might even say, "Don't bother Duke when he's eating; he doesn't like it." *This is a serious mistake.* As he grows up, this aggressive attitude will stick and Duke will mature into a terror who growls and snaps, at you and everyone else.

The suggestions found in these entries are not meant to be a substitute for the help of a professional trainer. These suggestions are not confrontational and are designed to keep you from provoking your dog into becoming more aggressive and biting you or others. They are general instructions to help your dog's attitude change in a gradual, casual way, a safe way.

The problem of aggression is complicated and serious and only a professional trainer can put together a training and behavior modification program that will work.

WHAT EVERY GOOD DOG OWNER MUST KNOW

You love your dog; you want everyone else to love her, too—right? One way to make your pet the most popular dog in town is to *clean up after her*—always, thoroughly, every time, and everywhere you go. Clean up even when no one's looking, even when you're the only one on the beach or in the woods. *Clean up.* Carry old plastic bags with you, or use a scoop—whatever works for you. But never, never neglect this crucial responsibility.

GETTING STARTED

THE COLLAR

There are three types of dog collars: buckle collars, slip collars (like choke chains), and pinch-prong collars. Buckle collars don't tighten automatically, are made of nylon or leather, and may have a quick-release snap. Slip collars tighten when pulled and are made of nylon, leather, or metal. Do not use a prong collar; it could injure your dog. It should be used by professional trainers only.

Keep a buckle collar with an ID tag on your dog at all times. Never leave a choke chain on him or tie him up with one, as it could get hooked on something, and your dog could choke. If you are starting out with a puppy from seven weeks to six months old, us a soft buckle collar. Never put a choke chain on a puppy, as it can panic or injure him.

The buckle collar should fit snugly so that your dog can't slip out of it, but it should be loose enough to swivel around his neck easily. Usually a two-finger gap is adequate. Puppies grow very quickly, so check the collar weekly to make sure it isn't getting too tight. Make sure your dog is comfortable in his collar. If it is too thick, stiff, or rough, it will cause irritation.

The choke chain is a type of slip collar that tightens when pulled. Your dog responds to the pressure on his neck as well as to the twangy sound the collar makes when it is zipped tight. Choke chains, when used incorrectly, can hurt your dog. Be very careful not to tighten the chain so much that you choke your dog. The choke chain is useful, but it must be used sensitively.

A choke chain can be quite effective if your dog pulls you around on his buckle collar. He may still try to pull you around on his choke chain, however, so it is important for you to learn how to use the choke chain before you try it out on the dog. Practice walking your dog indoors on a loose leash attached to his buckle collar until you have mastered the correct walking techniques before you switch to a choke chain.

Choke chains come sized in 2-inch increments and in different thicknesses. The chain needs to rest comfortably at the base of your dog's neck, and when you pull it into a gently snug position, there should be 2 to 3 extra inches of chain. (If you have a hairy dog that gets clipped regularly, you might need two collars for the different hair lengths.) Start with a chain of medium thickness.

When the choke chain is on correctly, the leash snap will zing it tight and allow it to loosen instantly. If it is on backwards, it will catch on your dog's throat and not release. This will cause your dog discomfort, may cause him to gag or cough from the constant pressure, and could harm his sensitive throat. With your dog at your left side, lower the chain through one of the rings, spread open the collar, and slip it over your dog's head with the loose ring hanging down to the right of the dog's neck. Stand in front of him and pull it snug. If it forms the letter *P* on the dog's neck (a rather sloppy *P*, that is), it is on correctly. If it forms the number 9, it is on backward. Turn it around.

WRONG WAY

RIGHT WAY

THE LEASH

L eashes come in varying lengths, materials, thicknesses, and
styles. It is important to select one that's comfortable for your
dog and for you to hold.

Pick a leash that is strong and supple with smooth edges. Pull it
through your hand; it should not feel slippery. Leather leashes are
strong and supple and are available in a variety of thicknesses.
Leashes made of cotton webbing are inexpensive, practical, light-
weight, and easy to grip; they come in lengths from 4 to 50 feet.
Chain leashes can be very hard on your hands.

For basic obedience training, you'll need a 6-foot leash. For training and playtimes, you'll also need a 30- to 50-foot line so your dog
can romp in the park.

The metal snap at the end of the leash should be the smallest size
that will safely hold your dog. Large snaps can whack her in the jaw,
especially if she's small. A large dangling snap also tends to pull a
choke chain too snug, and your dog will not appreciate having to lug
a huge, heavy snap around.

You can also buy spring-loaded leashes that uncoil from a casing
that you hold. These leashes allow you to walk your dog on a longer
line without worrying about tangling. City dogs and their owners love

these leashes because they allow more freedom of movement. While you walk, your dog can trot next to you or sprint in front of you. *Be sure you are adept with the controls* before you use this type of leash, or your dog could dash out into the street or trip someone before you figure out which button to push!

Since the spring-loaded leash will pull slightly on your dog's collar, it is best to use a buckle collar instead of a choke chain so that your dog will not get used to pulling on his choke chain.

If your dog grabs his leash between his teeth, pull it through his mouth very quickly before he can clamp down on it. The leash will scrape his mouth unpleasantly, and this will discourage him from grabbing it again.

TEACHING THE BASIC COMMANDS

SIT

The sit is the easiest command to teach. This command is useful when you want to get your dog's attention. You can also use the sit command before getting in and out of cars, at curbs, and at the front door. And it is useful when changing collars, administering medicine, greeting people, and giving your dog a treat.

Two methods of teaching the sit are explained here. Use whichever one works best with your dog.

The Hands-On Method

1. Place your dog on your left side with her head near your leg. Tell her, "Sheba, sit," and give her the hand signal, which is an upward sweep of your forearm (bending at the elbow) that starts at your side and ends at your shoulder. Then use your hands to guide her to a sitting position. Pull up and back on her collar with your right hand; with your left thumb and index finger push down gently just in front of her hipbones.

2. As soon as your dog begins to respond to the pressure and lower her rear end, stop pushing and pulling and let her finish the sit

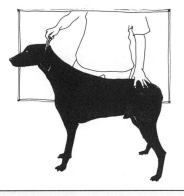

TEACHING THE SIT

on her own. The instant she is seated, tell her "Good sit!" and scratch her rump a little. Sound sincerely pleased when you praise her; remember she is learning a new language, and that's not easy. Show her you are proud.

3. Practice five or six sits in a row and then take a break. Give your dog a little calming massage to her neck and toss a toy for her a few times, then practice some more. Each sit session can last up to ten minutes (less for puppies), including the play and massage time. Practice several times a day to keep the command fresh in her mind. As your dog improves, you will be able to lighten up your hand cues, and she will respond to your voice alone.

Here are some of the problems you may encounter when teaching the sit command. Each problem is followed by a solution.

- *Your dog seems baffled or frightened by the collar cue and resists it.* Use your right hand as a substitute for the collar. Put gentle pressure on her throat with the edge of your hand between your thumb and index finger, and lift your hand slightly, raising her head. As she sits, praise her and scratch her throat. This will help her learn to accept the collar cue and learn to sit; you can also add a food treat to this if it helps.

- *Your dog is small, frightened, or very energetic, or it is hard for you to bend over.* Practice the sit command while your dog is on a countertop or table, but be sure to put a nonslip rug under her.

- *Your dog resists your hip cue.* This can happen if your cue is a push with the palm of your hand instead of a tap with your finger; your dog may think she's getting rubbed. Also, if you forget to cue her collar and just push her rump down, she will wait every time for you to push her rump, because that's the only signal she gets.

- *You can't get her to lower her rump.* Slide your left hand over her rump and down her back legs, tucking her back legs gently under her so she bends them at the knees. She will have no choice but to sit. Then, give her lots of praise. As always, let her know you adore her.

- *The choke chain scares your dog, and she refuses to sit.* Do not pull on the slip ring (the loose ring the leash attaches to) to signal for the sit. Instead, put your hand through the whole collar and cue her by tugging the collar gently upward. Once your dog understands the collar cue, you can signal her by pulling gently on either the slip ring or the leash.

- *Your dog sits sloppily on one hip.* Some short-legged, long-bodied dogs—basset hounds and dachshunds, for example—and some large-breed pups are more comfortable sitting on one hip. If this more casual style leads to your dog lying down, then you must insist on the straighter sit. Otherwise, let your dog sit in a relaxed and comfortable position.

The Hands-Off Method

The hands-off method of teaching your dog to sit combines food with the collar cue. This method is useful for puppies, dogs who are nervous about having their hindquarters handled, and dogs who just plain don't want to sit down. This also works for people who have trouble bending over to reach their dogs.

In your left hand, hold your dog on a gathered-up leash, and in your right, have a treat. Your dog should be on your left side with her head by your knee in the heel position. Tell her, "Sheba, sit," and lift up both of your hands at the same time. With your left hand, pull up on the collar while you sweep your right hand up past her nose so she can smell the treat. End up with your right hand above her head. As soon as she sits, praise her: "Good sit!" and give her the treat.

SIT-STAY

In the sit-stay your goal is to have your dog remain seated until you tell her she can get up. This command is useful whenever you want your dog to remain in one spot.

To teach the sit-stay, put a collar and a leash on your dog. Be sure she understands the sit command before you begin the sit-stay exercise.

1. With your dog seated by your left leg, gather the entire leash in your left hand and pull it straight up behind your dog's head until you are putting slight pressure on her throat. Tell her, "Stay," in a firm voice. *Do not use her name or she may think you are calling her and move toward you.*

2. At the same time, with your right hand give her the hand signal by sweeping your open right hand toward her face and stopping 8 to 12 inches from her nose. Don't put your hand any closer or she may try to sniff it, and don't block her eyes. It is important to be able to make eye contact with her.

THE HAND SIGNAL FOR THE STAY

3. Step back an arm's length without allowing the collar to lose contact with her neck. Keep giving her the hand signal and remind her verbally to stay. Hold her just firmly enough for her to understand that you can control her, but don't pull her so hard that she's half strangling; some dogs actually require very little contact. Be observant. Count to five and release her by saying, "Okay! Good girl!" in a happy voice. Pat your legs and invite her over for some praise, bending down to greet her.

4. Practice several sit-stays in a row. Then take a short play and massage break and repeat the exercise several more times. End her first session on a successful, well-done sit-stay.

Make sure your tone of voice is clear. Use a cautioning tone for the command and a happy tone for the release. If she needs reassuring while she's in the sit-stay, tell her in a calm, cautioning tone, "You're good, you stay."

The Advanced Sit-Stay

Always start an advanced sit-stay session by reviewing a couple of easy stays. As she improves, slowly increase the amount of time she's in the sit-stay, but remain only an arm's length away and hold the leash up over her head.

When she is steady on the stay, calmly walk a half circle around in front of her. Move slowly and as you walk, remind her periodically, with the hand signal and your voice, to stay. Next, walk a full circle around her, but don't try too much too soon; make sure she remains steady before you add the distraction of movement. Eventually, you can practice the advanced sit-stay on a long line.

As you add distance and movement, keep most of the slack out of the leash so you can control her instantly if she breaks from the stay. If you are too slow to correct her, she will continue to break and will never learn. As she gets steadier in her stays, you can be her first distraction. Scuffle your feet as you walk around her, then skip. When she is steady with that, you can introduce her to other distractions, such as another dog (a well-mannered one), another person, or events in the great outdoors.

When your dog can hold a sit-stay for one full minute while you are at the end of a 6-foot leash, you can use a slightly more complicated release to end the stay. This release teaches her to hold her position until you return to her side and is especially useful for shy dogs, dogs who couldn't care less about being trained, and dogs who play keep-away and are hard to catch.

When you want to end your dog's sit-stay, return to her side, cautioning her to stay. Stand in the heel position without touching her and make sure she doesn't move. Pause for a few seconds, tell her, "Stay," and take a giant step to your right. Wait a few seconds and release her with a happy "Okay! Good girl!" so that she must come to you for her praise. Once your dog is capable of doing this, you should use this release for all of her stay commands, unless you are going directly into the come command.

Here are some problems you may encounter when teaching the sit-stay. Each problem is followed by a solution.

- *Your dog fidgets.* Tell her, "No! Stay," and tug upward on the leash. If she gets up, tell her, "No!" and gently tug her back to her sit-stay spot with the leash, but keep your hands off her. Command her to sit and stay, give her the hand signal, and step away immediately. Remember to be gentle when you pull her back to her spot.

- *She is very wiggily and excitable.* Give her a calming massage and practice a sit-stay without leaving her side. Next, try a sit-stay while standing directly in front of her; always move very slowly and remind her to stay. As she improves, you can increase the time she needs to remain in the sit-stay position, as well as increasing your distance from her.

- *Your dog does not want to remain seated.* Sitting may be painful for her; she may have a sore back or hips. Young, large-bodied dogs often prefer to lie down and will voluntarily sit only for short periods. Observe her when she's not in training and see how long she sits on her own. If you think she is in pain, take her to your veterinarian. If she seems quite comfortable sitting on her own then require that she do so for you until she learns to pay attention to what you tell her. Then teach her the down-stay command so she can relax.

- *She seems scared and lies down.* Don't haul her up by the collar—this will only frighten her more. Get her up with enthusiasm, saying, "Come on, sit." Have her sit, remain by her side, give her a calming massage, and scratch her chest. This will help her remain seated. Then, while massaging her, pull up a little bit on her collar, telling her to stay. Count to five, release her with a happy "Okay! Good girl!" and then repeat the exercise.

- *Your dog makes a big game out of the sit-stay.* She will collapse and roll around. Pull on the leash and say, "No! Sit!" If necessary, hoist her up with your hands. Immediately plunk her into a sit, steady her with the leash, and tell her to stay. The minute she thinks of collapsing, give her a firm reminder tug to the collar and a firm "Stay!" Count to ten and release her.

HEEL

Once you have taught your dog to heel, he will follow faithfully at your heels. You will be the pack leader heading down the trail, and your dog will be a subordinate pack member who must follow you. The heel is an important command, as it requires your dog to learn to control himself while he's in motion next to you.

To teach the heel, put a leash and a collar on your dog. The leash is necessary for control and for giving him the leash snap as you signal him to stay by your side.

There are various techniques for teaching your dog to heel, and the variations depend on your dog's attitude and temperament and your skills as a teacher. The method taught here involves a great deal of encouragement and praise. By praising your dog when he is heeling correctly, you are giving him the feedback necessary to let him know what pleases you. The more pleasant you make it for your dog to follow you, the more natural it will be for him to want to stay by your side.

The most important thing to remember when teaching your dog to heel is to keep the leash slack unless you are giving your dog a leash snap as a signal to get back into position. You will tighten the leash for only an instant, as a reminder to your dog. He must then exhibit some self-control and remember to maintain the heel position. If you hold him back with a tight leash, he won't have to use any self-control and he won't learn anything.

It is best to start all training indoors, where there are few distractions. Have your dog walk with you through the house—down hallways and around chairs and tables. Then work your way outside, first into the backyard, then out to the sidewalk. If your dog is used to being outdoors, begin your practice outside in his pen or yard, where everything is familiar. Keep the leash loose at all times. Maintain just enough slack in the line to keep the choke chain loose on the dog's neck.

In order for the heel command to take, it is important that you always base the leash in your right hand, with your dog on your left side. Drop the leash loop over your right thumb, using your thumb as a hook, and make extra loops around your thumb until you get the correct amount of leash played out. Grab the whole wad in your fist, making sure it feels comfortable and secure. When your left hand takes the leash, make sure your palm is facing down and toward you. Your pinky should be facing the dog and your thumb should be up.

Hold your right hand near your belly button and test the amount of slack in the leash. It should hang down and droop in a little loop

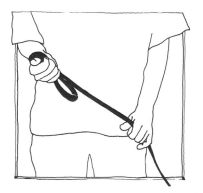

HOLDING THE LEASH DURING HEELING

just beneath the dog's collar. Test its snapping action by pulling your hand out to the right. You should be able to bring the collar into contact with your dog's neck with an easy motion. If your dog wears a choke chain, keep an eye on it; the rings should dangle together down by his throat, and the collar must remain fully open and not be twisted or partially pulled up. There must be enough slack in the line for the snap to hang down freely.

Your left hand should be relaxed at your side. You can use it to give leash snaps, to pat your leg encouragingly, or to scratch your dog's head (or your nose, if need be). Hold your right hand near your belly button in a ready position, or relaxed by your side. Keep your hands as low as possible when you do the leash snaps, so that your dog is tugged at head level rather than being pulled upward. This is especially important with little dogs.

Starting the Heel

1. With your dog seated on your left side, cheerfully tell her, "Muffy, heel!" and slap your left leg encouragingly. This leg slap is also your hand signal. Start walking, leading with either leg, and immediately praise her for following you: "Good girl! Good heel!" Keep her interested in you by talking to her happily as you walk, making it sound like fun. Pat your leg frequently or give her ears an occasional scratch as you walk; your happy patter will make her want to follow you and will let her know she's doing it right.

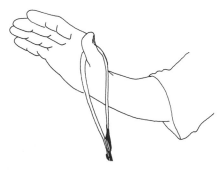

ALLOWING ENOUGH SLACK IN THE LINE #1

ALLOWING ENOUGH SLACK IN THE LINE #2

2. Keep your dog's nose even with your leg as you walk. When she starts to inch ahead of you, do a leash snap and tell her "No!" in a firm voice at the same time. Then pat your leg and encourage her: "Heel! Good heel, good Muffy!" If she needs more encouragement, scratch her head. Every time she starts to quicken her pace and forge ahead, repeat the entire sequence. Remember to praise her. After she gets the hang of heeling, you can just say, "No!" without the leash snap and she'll probably respond. If not, use the leash as a backup to your voice.

3. Change your pace from normal to slow to fast, using a calming voice to slow her down ("Easy, girl") or an excited voice and a few leg slaps to speed up ("Let's go—hurry!"). These changes make heeling more interesting and teach your dog to adjust her pace to yours. Change your direction frequently as well; zigzag around so she never knows what you will do next.

4. As you practice with your dog, anticipate any distraction that might lead her off course, and encourage her with great enthusiasm to remain by your side. If encouragement doesn't work, try a firm "No!" or "Leave it!" and a leash snap if necessary. Praise her immediately for responding.

5. Come to a halt slowly so that your dog will have some warning. If she does not stop when you halt, give her a gentle leash snap as a reminder. Make sure she stops right next to your leg.

6. If your dog has learned the sit command, incorporate it into her heeling work. Do short drills where you require her to sit after heeling for a while. Don't forget the constant praise.

Right Turn and Right U-Turn

Before you turn, say, "Muffy, heel!" Slap your leg to get her attention and to warn her of a directional change; then pause, turn, and praise her for following. If she doesn't follow you, give her a gentle leash snap to get her attention; then praise her for catching up. Every time you turn right, follow this sequence.

Left Turn and Left U-Turn

Before your turn left (toward her), tell her, "Muffy, heel!" and tug back with the leash to slow her down and get her out of your way. If she has trouble getting out of your way, she was probably too far forward when you began the turn, and it's okay to *gently* bump her out of the way with your left leg.

When you first start training her, turn when she is in the correct heel position, rather than when she's forging ahead. Once she understands what's expected of her you can spring surprise turns on her.

Using Food as an Incentive

If you've having a hard time getting your dog to follow you or if you are teaching a puppy, you'll need to up the ante by using food as an incentive.

Settle the leash in your left hand comfortably and securely. Leave enough slack to form a loop beneath the collar when your arm is by your side. Hide a food treat in your right hand and let your dog have a taste.

Next, say, "Muffy, heel." Make a pass near her nose with the food, and start walking. Hold the food near your left hip, so that in order for her to keep her eye on the treat she has to walk slightly behind you. Every so often, while she is heeling nicely, pass her a treat, and don't forget to praise her happily as you walk. If she lunges at the food, hold it farther from her face or give her a leash snap. Before you change your direction, say, "Muffy, heel," slap your leg, lure her with the food, and give her a nibble.

Walking Styles

Making your dog heel constantly on a walk is boring for you and for her. Whenever possible, play out more line and let her walk on a loose leash so she can sniff and explore. If she begins to pull you, signal her with a leash snap just before she gets a chance to. Make your changes in walking style obvious. Tell her, "Okay, go sniff," and play out the line. When you want to return to the heel position, bring her to your side, have her sit, and calm her by stroking her slowly. Then formally set off at a heel, saying "Muffy, heel!"

Once your dog is trained to heel, you can put the entire leash in your left hand and adjust the length to allow you to swing your arm without yanking your dog around. Then you can stride down the street, arms swinging freely, while your dog keeps pace with you.

If your dog does not respond to this teaching method and continues to pull you around, ignoring your encouragement, your leash snaps, and your treats, you must resort to a firmer method. See "Leash, pulling on," in "Dog Problems from A to Z."

DOWN

In teaching the down command, your goal is to have your dog lie down the instant you give the command, regardless of any distractions. It is an excellent way to interrupt your dog when he is about to do something annoying or dangerous, and when combined with the down-stay, it provides a way to keep him still.

Because the down is a submissive position, many dogs don't like it, while others are very insecure about it. Your dog, whether he likes the command or not, must learn that you are the pack leader, and you're in charge.

There are two methods for teaching—one uses food; the other does not—both are hands-on techniques and must be done with compassion, patience, and love in order to foster trust and respect. It is most important not to create fear or resentment in your dog when teaching this command.

Using Food as an Incentive

The food-incentive method of teaching the down is useful for puppies, shy dogs, older dogs, dominant dogs, and stubborn dogs.

Your dog will be receiving several cues at once. In addition to luring him with a treat, you'll be teaching him to respond to pressure on his collar or shoulders and you'll be giving him a hand signal—a sweeping motion of your right hand that starts above your dog's head and finishes on the floor. At first it is important to sweep your hand all the way down and tap the floor, but as your dog becomes familiar with the hand signal, you will not have to go all the way down.

1. Have your dog on your left side in the sit position. Hide a treat in your right hand. Squat or sit on the floor, to the dog's right, put your left hand on your dog's shoulders (the base of the dog's neck, where it meets the back), and rest it there. Tell your dog, "Max, down," and swing your right hand, palm down, from above his head down past his nose, slowly luring his nose down to the floor near his toes. Then move your hand slowly along the floor away from your dog, sliding it in a straight line away from his nose. As your hand moves away and your dog follows, sniffing the treat, he will probably plop down. As soon as he does, turn your hand over and feed him the treat, telling him, "Good down!" Give his back a good scratch to help him stay down for a bit.

2. As he lowers himself, keep your left hand on his shoulders and gently follow him down with slight pressure. If he tries to stand up and walk to the treat, goes halfway down and stops, or lowers his front end but raises his rear, press on his shoulders and push him back down as he follows your enticing food lure. Be sure to praise any voluntary downward movement to let him know he's doing what you want.

3. Once he begins to understand that you want him to lie down, put your left hand on his collar, right under his chin and follow him down with the collar, making gentle contact with his neck. Don't yank or pull him down; let him learn to associate the gentle collar cue with lying down. If he stops partway down or tries to get back up, use the collar to keep him from rising. Then continue to entice him, saying, "Good boy. Good down. That's it, good down."

4. If your dog is a dachshund or another breed with very short legs, you'll find he doesn't have to lie down to reach the treat. You can help him by walking his little front legs out with your right hand, while your left hand gently presses down on his shoulders.

5. Practice this command several times in a row. Then take a play-massage break and practice again. Always end on a good note.

Teaching the Down Command Without Food

Use this technique if your dog doesn't seem interested in the food lure.

1. Squat down with your dog sitting next to you on your left side, and put your left hand on his collar under his throat. If you use a choke chain, put your hand through the whole collar rather than pulling on the ring that tightens the collar. With your right hand, give the hand signal, say, "Max, down," and tap the floor several times. Exert some light, steady downward pressure on the collar. If he drops his head and lowers himself, stop the pressure and let him go down on his own as you praise him. If he stops lowering himself, resume the gentle collar pressure until he is down. You can walk his front legs out one at a time as you pull downward, if necessary. Then, praise him calmly and scratch his back.

2. It might be necessary to keep your left arm over his shoulders as additional pressure. When you do so, slip your thumb through his collar, so you can use it to signal him downward.

3. If walking him one leg at a time isn't working, you may need to lift both legs at the same time and literally lower him to the floor. Be sure to do so gently and keep your arm over his shoulders. Once he is relaxed on the floor, lift your arm off his back and give him a scratch. Then let him get up. Remember to offer lots of encouragement and praise.

CORRECT HEELING POSITION

4. Practice five or six downs in a row, then take a break for a calming massage or a play session. Practice several more times and always end on a positive note.

Here are some problems you may encounter when teaching the down command. Each problem is followed by a solution.

- *Your dog makes a game out of the down command.* Make sure that he is getting enough exercise, especially before your practice sessions. Review heel, sit, and sit-stay until he settles down.

- *He gets nippy or tries to climb on you.* Correct him with a leash snap and a firm "No!" Settle him with a calming massage and try again.

HAND POSITIONS IN TEACHING THE DOWN

- *He is tense, trembling, or cowering.* Spend some time giving him a calming massage. When he relaxes and drops his head a little, give him the down command and continue massaging until he relaxes.

DOWN-STAY

Your goal in teaching the down-stay is to have your dog remain lying down until you tell her to get up. The command gets the attention of dogs who are so busy they don't seem to notice you exist. It also teaches them to stay calm, and it is useful when your dog wants to bark at things, since it is harder to bark lying down. Requiring your dog to remain in a down-stay is also a kind way to remind her of her subservient position in your pack and an excellent way to keep your dog still, yet let her be comfortable at the same time.

This command can be incorporated into daily life in many ways. She can learn to lie quietly at your feet while you read, eat, visit with friends, travel in the car, drink a cup of coffee at your favorite outdoor café, or attend an outdoor concert.

The hand signal for the down-stay is the same as that for the sit-stay—the open palm of your hand held near her face. After you give your dog the hand signal for down, immediately switch to the stay signal. Remember not to use your dog's name with any stay command, because she will think you are calling her and will be inclined to get up.

Here is how you teach the down-stay:

1. Once your dog is in the down position, immediately tell her "Stay," and remain squatting or sitting on the floor next to her. If she tries to get up, restrain her with a hand on her shoulders or her collar while you remind her to stay. Count to five, release her, saying, "Okay, good girl," and ask her to get up.

2. Repeat the entire sequence, staying right by her side. As she improves, move a few inches to your right, but stay close enough to restrain her if necessary. Do several very short stays; then try one for twenty seconds, and then thirty, all the while remaining next to her on the floor.

3. When she has learned to stay down for a full minute with you near her on the floor, stand up next to her. Get up slowly, reminding her to stay, and stand on the leash so she'll be restrained if she tries to get up. Make sure you allow enough slack so she can hold her head in a normal position. Make her stay for only thirty seconds, and then release her. If necessary, squat or sit on the floor with her to help her into the down position. This could take one training session or several.

Releasing Your Dog from the Down-Stay

When first practicing the down-stay, release your dog with a happy "Okay!" while you are at the end of the leash. This is a very easy release; as your dog improves, you can use an advanced release, as taught in the sit-stay section.

The Advanced Down-Stay

1. Build up your dog's stay time slowly, until she can do a three-minute down-stay with you standing a couple of feet away. When she understands the command and what is required of her, go to the end of the 6-foot leash and build up to a five-minute down-stay.

2. Next, walk in half-circles in front of her, then in full circles. Then skip or jog around her. When she can handle this without breaking from the down-stay, you are ready to practice out in the real world. Once outdoors, start with shorter, easier down-stays and build up to the five-minute down-stay.

3. Now it's time to work on longer down-stays. Start by practicing indoors with your dog at your feet while you sit in a chair or on the couch. Give her something to chew on and a comfortable place to lie. If she dozes, gently remind her when she awakens that she is still in a down-stay. Build her up gradually to a thirty-minute down-stay. Puppies under a year old should not be required to do a full thirty minutes, but you can work them toward it. Remember, always make sure to exercise your dog before asking her to do a long down-stay.

Here are some problems you may encounter when teaching the down-stay. Each problem is followed by a solution.

- *Your dog gets up before you've released her from the down-stay.* Rush to her and tell her "No!" If she has left her down-stay spot, return her to it by gently pulling her there with the leash and command her back into the down-stay. Don't pet her or say any kind words, but don't be rough with her, either. Your urgency in returning her to the spot and to the down position will let her know she has done something wrong.

- *She turns the exercise into a play session.* Do not stay on the floor with her. Instead, bend over her, and step on the leash the instant she lies down. Command her firmly to stay, and stand up straight. Allow enough slack in the line so she can hold her head in a normal, comfortable position.

- *She rolls on her back and looks silly.* Let her do so. She will get tired of that when she finds you are not trying to control her. When she rolls back onto her stomach, watch her closely and keep her from getting up by putting your foot on the leash. Keep your hands away from her, as touching her will only feed her folly. Require her to stay down long enough to focus and settle, and then release her.

- *Your dog is nervous about the down-stay.* Sit on the floor next to her while she's in her down-stay. Give her a calming massage, especially to her neck and ears and talk to her soothingly. When she relaxes, release her with "Okay!" and lots of praise. Then repeat the exercise.

COME

Your goal in teaching the come command is to have your dog return to your side immediately whenever you call her. Come is the most important command and the most difficult one for a dog to learn because you are asking her to give up her freedom. Its importance for safety purposes is obvious: if your dog dashes toward the street, being able to get her to come to your side could keep her from being hit by a car. The command also stops your dog from bothering other people or animals, chasing things, or running off to investigate off-limit areas.

You need to show your dog that coming to you is a pleasant experience. *Never call her and then punish her when she arrives,* no matter what she's done. If she's gotten herself into trouble, go to her. Don't call your dog to you and then do something unpleasant, such as scolding her or giving her medicine. Instead, go and get her and lead her back. Call her for things you know she finds pleasant— meals, treats, play sessions, car rides, walks. This way, she will regard coming to you as a pleasant experience.

There are two methods of teaching the come command—off-leash and on-leash. With the off-leash method, your dog learns to come to you because treats and praise await her. This method can be used at any time in a dog's life and is especially useful for puppies seven weeks old and up, young dogs, and shy dogs. It will teach any dog that coming to you has its rewards. The on-leash method also teaches your dog that praise and possibly treats await her, but that there will be unpleasant consequences, such as the leash snap, if she ignores the command.

The Off-Leash Method

The off-leash method is especially useful for puppies seven weeks old and up, young dogs, and shy dogs.

Start this lesson in the house. Hide some treats in your hand, and when your dog is not paying attention to you, flash the food under her nose and say, "Lady, come!" in a very happy voice. Run backward a few steps, praising gleefully to encourage your dog to follow you, saying "Good come! Good girl!"

Squat down to greet your dog, hug her, feed her the treat, and praise her, saying, "Good come! Good girl!" To teach her to come in close to you, hold the treat close to your body and as you feed her, scratch her back or rear end. This helps alleviate the snatch-the-food-and-run syndrome, and helps you gain her trust. After she has mastered this, practice the come command from a distance, making

COME: WELCOMING YOUR DOG

her run a little farther each time. For a hand signal at a distance, motion your dog with larger waves of your arms. Eventually you can do this in your yard or anywhere else you happen to be with your dog.

Call your dog when she least expects it. Make a game of calling her into and out of the house, up and down the stairs, and from hiding places. Call her to you when she is playing with another dog, but start from very close, to keep it easier. In areas where you can't let her loose, practice on a 50-foot cord. Keep the lessons short.

If you want your dog to come to others, have them practice with you. Call the dog back and forth between you—one at a time, of course. If she runs to someone who hasn't called her, that person must ignore her and let someone else call her. This way she will learn to respond to the command rather than to view humans as convenient food dispensers. Give her the treat every time she comes during the first few training sessions. Then skip the treat every so often and give her a good rubbing instead.

The On-Leash Method

Before starting to use this method, you must teach the other commands. This on-leash method is useful for any dog who does not come when called and for whom the food incentive is useless. Puppies should be at least four months old before you try this method; at that age, just a very gentle leash snap is all that's needed for your puppy to respond to you.

Put your dog on a 6-foot leash and let her casually wander about. Keep the leash from getting tangled in her legs and try to maintain a direct line to her neck, keeping just enough slack in the leash so that she doesn't feel it. When she is totally distracted by something, surprise her by saying happily, "Lady come!" Sound urgent. If she turns and looks at you, immediately tell her, "Good girl, good come," and run backward, clapping your hands and praising her as she comes to you. Bend down and greet her with open arms and lots of hugs and scratches; you can also slip her a treat if you'd like.

If she ignores your command, give her a leash snap to get her attention and to turn her head toward you. Praise her instantly for looking at you, repeat the command, and bring her all the way in, saying, "Good come! Good girl! Come on, Lady. Good Lady!"

If your dog stops coming, veers off course, or goes right past you, stop the praise and give her a firm "No!" Then repeat the command and bring her in with the praise. If telling her "No!" doesn't get her attention, add a leash snap. Alternate between the praise and the correction as you make her come to you. Don't grab at her; encourage her instead. When you give her the leash snap make sure you don't inadvertently drag her halfway back to you; the leash snap signals your dog to look at you and then come to you voluntarily. Remember, your dog is your companion and playmate; don't haul her in like a fish on a line.

Once you get the hang of the come command on the 6-foot lead, go to a 15- or 30-foot line, and then a 50-foot line. Once your dog responds well on the long line, begin to make the transition to coming off-leash. Practice the come on the long line several times. Then let go of it and let her drag it around; she will assume you have the end of it when you call her. If she doesn't respond, step on the cord. As she gets better about coming, slowly shorten the cord.

Using Come with Other Commands

You can practice the come command from a sit-stay once your dog is steady in her stays. You can also have your dog sit after you call her to you, but have her do so only after she learns how much fun it is to come to you.

THE TOOLS OF THE TRADE

T he tools discussed in the following pages give you several ways to get your dog's attention and communicate with him. They are essential in helping you correct his mistakes and prevent them from happening again.

YOUR VOICE AND YOUR HANDS

T he most natural communication tools are always available: your voice and your hands. You can use your hands as a backup for your voice when necessary. When used for correction, your hands transmit a message to your dog that he must stop what he's doing, pay attention, and listen to you—now! Slow hands that perform calming massages will tell your dog that you care about his well-being.

YOUR VOICE

Your voice is one of your most useful communication tools. It transmits your feelings, moods, emotions, and desires. A happy upbeat tone always gets a dog's tail wagging. It's a clear signal to your dog that you are pleased with him. A low, serious voice elicits a more subdued response. The tail is lowered, the ears drop, and your dog wears an "uh-oh" look. Your voice can also express gratitude, apology, concern, caution, love, and many other feelings.

Because your tone of voice transmits your feelings to your dog more clearly than the actual words you use, it is important to become aware of how you sound to your dog. Use a *firm* tone to gain your dog's respect and cooperation. Depending on the situation, you can use a commanding tone (authoritative but friendly), a correcting tone (firm, serious, attention-getting, no-nonsense), a praising tone (sincere and appreciative), a cautioning tone, or an encouraging tone. You can also sound silly, happy, loving, soothing, or apologetic.

Use the commanding and correcting tones to get your dog's attention. They are lower-pitched and come from your gut. Do not sound questioning; you are not asking your dog to stop; you are telling her. In contrast, the praising tones are higher in pitch. Using distinctive voice tones makes it easier for your dog to understand you. By changing your voice you imitate the natural sounds that dogs make. For instance, growling is a low sound, whereas a dog's playful tones are higher.

Men and women often have different problems communicating with their dogs. Because of the difference in male and female voices, it is common for women to have difficulty sounding firm enough and for men to have difficulty sounding soft and encouraging, resulting in a dog who doesn't take the woman seriously and who is intimidated by the man.

Your voice must reflect your sincere belief that your dog is intelligent and capable of learning. If you have any doubts, they will be evident in your voice, and your dog will ignore you. Your correcting voice must reflect your intent to back up what you say with action, if need be. If your dog hears willfulness in your voice, he will be more inclined to take heed.

The words you use are also important. Dogs can learn phrases and individual words. In fact, dogs who help the disabled can learn up to sixty commands and phrases. If you are consistent with your phrases and repeat the same thing over and over again, your dog will begin to understand what you are saying. When you're housebreaking your dog, for example, everyone in the household must use exactly the same words. "Go outside?" means the same as "Go potty?" but your dog will be utterly confused if you use both phrases. You must be consistent with your words if you want your dog to understand you. Choose one phrase and use it all the time.

When teaching the formal obedience commands, keep them short and simple. If your dog is about to run into the street, you don't have time to discuss it. You need your dog to respond to a one-word command: "Come."

The volume at which you speak to your dog is also important. Dogs have excellent hearing and appreciate being talked to in a normal, conversational voice. If you always yell at your dog, he will tune you out just to protect his ears. You won't have much recourse in emergencies if your dog is already used to hearing you yell, but if you speak in a normal voice to your dog, he will pay attention when you do increase the volume. Sometimes all you may need is a soft-spoken "Hey!" to get your dog's attention. Try putting him through his obedience routine, speaking only in a whisper, and notice how attentive he'll be.

By the way, it's perfectly okay to talk to your dog! The comical image of the little old lady talking to her poodle is actually a good one to imitate. Those ladies often have very intelligent, responsive dogs with large vocabularies, who actually listen to their owners.

Like your voice, your hands are useful communications tools. As a backup to your voice, they can help you correct your dog, welcome him, signal him, or soothe him. By learning to use your hands for the massage, you'll have an effective way to calm your dog.

THE CALMING MASSAGE

The calming massage will help your dog relax and focus. It is also a bonding process that builds mutual trust, respect, and appreciation. Dogs, like humans, can feel stress and tension in their bodies. By relieving your dog's tension and soothing his aches and pains through massage, you can tell him that you care about him and that his needs are very important to you.

If you practice the massage every day, your dog will respond easily to your calming touch, and this will enable you to calm him down quickly when you need to. He will feel your familiar hands on him and decide that maybe chasing the cat isn't all that important—especially if, after you correct him, you start working on that knot of tension in his neck. In the training sequence, first you correct him, then you give an obedience command, then you help him calm down with the massage.

Massage is also a good way to get to know your dog's body and to check for growths, skin problems, fleas, ticks, or injuries. If your dog reacts with pain or discomfort while you are massaging, be especially gentle. Back off from these areas and work around them. If you suspect a lump or injury, see your veterinarian.

Find a quiet place with no distractions—your living room, den, or bedroom, or any quiet place in the house. Set aside at least thirty minutes so that you won't feel rushed. Put on some mellow music, lower the lights, and let everything else fade into the background.

Make sure you're both comfortable. If you have a large dog, sit on a chair or couch with your dog seated on the floor in front of you, facing away from you, and braced between your legs. If your dog is small, he can sit on your lap or next to you on the couch. If he wants to lie down after you start the neck massage, fine, since you want him to relax anyway. If he lies down and starts to play, get him up and have him sit until he understands what's going on.

Breathe deeply as you massage your dog. Sighs are contagious—like yawns. Tension is released through breathing and any knots you find in your dog's body will be likely to loosen up if you breathe deeply yourself.

Begin with a warm-up neck massage. Start with a soft touch, slowly scratching and rubbing the hair on your dog's neck. Then cup your hand to fit his neck and slowly slide your dog's skin around over the underlying muscles. You must press gently but firmly enough so that you're not just rubbing his hair but moving his skin as you slide your hand over his neck muscles.

CALMING MASSAGE: GETTING COMFORTABLE

This slow, gentle start is important for dogs whose necks are stiff from their collars or from pulling on the leash. Certain breeds, such as terriers and whippets, are tighter-skinned than others and require a very gentle start. This is true also for any dog that has been abused or has aggressive tendencies. You will know if you are doing it right, because your dog will relax and may begin to lower his head.

As your dog relaxes under your touch, *gently* grasp the loose skin on the scruff of his neck and knead it slowly, opening and closing your hand as you move your fingers in a circular motion. Rub the loose skin together between your fingers and then slide it over his muscles. If your touch is right, your dog will close his eyes or lower his head. Ease over to new areas as he relaxes. Massage the base of

MASSAGING YOUR DOG'S NECK

his ears, rubbing the ear leather, much as you do when you administer ear drops. If your nails are short, massage just inside the ear, along all the curly ridges and on the inside of the ear leather. Your touch on the acupuncture points in this area is very therapeutic and relaxing for your dog. Work your way up to his forehead muscles and move slowly down his back, loosening the area along his spine. Get him used to having his legs and feet and toes massaged; this will make it easier to cut his nails when the time comes for that.

Be creative. There is no wrong way to do a healing massage if your dog likes what you're doing.

Massaging a Restless Dog

Initially some dogs will be too restless to sit still for a long massage, so start with a shorter one. One way to calm a dog and get him ready for a massage is to exercise him thoroughly beforehand. If your dog is still too wired to sit still, put a leash on his collar and make him sit and stay while you introduce him to the massage. If he sits still for a few minutes, praise him and let him get up and move around a bit, then try again. As his muscles respond, he'll hold still for longer and longer. If he doesn't want to be massaged the whole time, spend quiet time alone with him anyway to help him calm down.

To control your dog and calm him down anytime and any place, put a leash on him and keep him on your left side, in a sit-stay. Put the leash in your right hand, for control, and use your left hand to

CALMING AND CONTROLLING A RESTLESS DOG

massage your dog. If he acts up, give him a leash snap or scruff grip; then ease back into the massage. If he's small, you can do the same on the couch or on your lap. Remember: control with one hand, and massage with the other, switching hands when necessary.

Using Slow Hands

Petting your dog *slowly* will help her slow down and focus. This is especially important if your dog is very wild or mouthy. Slow hands are hands that are aware of how they are affecting your dog. They are often used after you have gained control over your dog and must help her settle down and relax.

Slow down the whole petting process so that you hands transmit calmness and control. Approach your dog slowly. Stroke your dog firmly enough so that her skin is pulled along slightly under your hand. A stroke that begins just behind the eyes and goes down over the ears, smoothing the ears into a lower, relaxed position is especially calming. If you have a dog with stiff upright ears—a Scottie, for example, or a German shepherd—she might not like to have her ears slicked back. If this is the case, avoid smoothing down your dog's ears.

Be careful not to bonk your dog or pat her too hard on her head. Sadly, most dogs will tolerate being hit this way because this is better than no touch at all. After a while, however, your dog may shy away

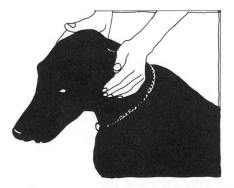

LONG, SLOW STROKING TECHNIQUE

from your hands and the jarring greeting they deliver. Always make sure your pats are soothing and caring.

BE CAREFUL NOT TO HIT TOO HARD

THE LEASH SNAP

The leash snap is another tool you can use to communicate with your dog. Not all dogs are the same, of course, and you must choose the correct tool for your dog's temperament. If you have a sensitive dog, a very minor interruption is all that's necessary— perhaps a tiny shake of the shaker can or a gentle tug on the leash. A more hard-headed dog will need a stronger message such as the leash snap. Use the minimum amount of correction necessary to get your dog's attention.

In order for your dog to notice the leash snap, it must be preceded and followed by a slack leash so that it is taut for only a split second. This applies whether you are standing casually with your dog or walking along.

The leash snap is used when your dog is about to pull you, jump on you or others, or bark. Whenever she's about to jerk you, you must jerk her first, so that she will learn to keep an eye on you and not pull. When the leash is slack before and after you snap, your dog will notice the snap on her neck, and the faster the signal, the more she'll notice it.

Always be consistent with your dog. "Leave it" is a good command to use when you want your dog to ignore something. "Off" is good when she jumps on someone or something. At other times the leash snap, executed silently, is more effective. It is important to feel comfortable handling the leash and to know just how to snap it. If your timing is right and you snap the leash just before your dog misbehaves, you do not have to snap very hard; your dog's neck muscles are relaxed and you are taking him by surprise. *Your must be sure that you are not hurting your dog.* Never tighten the collar to the point that he is choking, and *never, ever hang him by his collar,* even if his hind feet are on the ground.

Perfect the quick arm-hand movement by practicing before you put the leash on your dog. An effective way to practice this is to loop the handle of the leash over a doorknob. Then take hold of the snap end with your left hand, stand back a bit so there is some slack in the line, and try to flick the leash handle off the doorknob. This doesn't duplicate the leash snap action exactly, but it does help you learn how to move your hand very quickly in the snap-and-release motion.

Snap the leash only as firmly as you need to in order to get your dog's attention—a teeny bit harder than the yank she was about to dish out to you. This takes skilled handling, especially if you have a small or sensitive dog, since it doesn't take much to signal them. *Never overcorrect.*

With some dogs you will have to do several consecutive leash snaps before they will stop lunging and notice you. Give such dogs regular calming massages to soften the neck-area tissue and resensitize them.

A snap will turn into a pull if it is done too slowly and the pressure is held for more than a split second (two or three seconds is too long). A pull gives your dog time to tighten her neck muscles, resist, and pull, and any steady pressure on your part will be met with steady resistance from her. Don't try to pull your dog back toward you. Just send a signal down her leash through the snap to her collar.

If you are too slow and she pulls the leash tight before you have a chance to snap it, deliberately give your dog some slack, then give her a leash snap. Be patient with yourself; your reflexes will quicken with practice.

LETTING THE LEASH SNAP TURN INTO A PULL

THE SCRUFF GRIP

The scruff grip is a hands-on way to disrupt undesirable behavior and get your dog's attention. It is useful when you need to nab your dog in the act of doing something he shouldn't be doing. If you are near him and don't have a leash or collar on him, you can use the scruff grip. He will understand this action because dogs do it to each other. When you grasp your dog by the scruff of his neck, your hands are duplicating the jaws of another dog. This sends a signal to your dog—you literally have him by the neck. *You must end every scruff grip by easing off slowly into a calming massage, so his neck will feel soothed after the correction, and so he knows he can come back into your good graces.*

Here's how it's done: Simply grasp a large handful of loose skin at the back of your dog's neck, tighten your grip, twist your hand a little, and pull up very slowly. As soon as your dog freezes, looks up at you, or puts his ears back submissively or questioningly, slowly let go and ease back into the calming massage. If your dog has a lot of loose skin on his neck, you may have to tighten your grip quite a bit before he will feel it. Make sure you do not grip too tightly. Better to undercorrect than to overcorrect.

Instead of gripping the loose skin on his neck, you can simply hold your dog still with your hands on his shoulders, but make sure your

THE SCRUFF GRIP

fingers are not pressing on his throat. Release your grip slowly and ease into the calming massage. This method works well for small dogs, puppies, sensitive or timid dogs, and the finer-bodied breeds, such as some terriers and sight hounds, who have tighter skin and minimal body fat.

This type of correction entails nabbing your dog quickly and gripping him for a few seconds while you lecture him firmly. The more serious the crime, the longer you should grip and lecture—perhaps twenty seconds for a major offense. Glare at him and maintain eye contact as you lecture.

Loosen your hold slowly, just as another dog would do, and ease into a calming neck massage. If he acts up again, repeat the scruff grip or shoulder grip, returning to the calming massage once he gets your message.

It is important to praise your dog as you calm him. This lets him know that stopping the bad behavior has pleased you. If you fail to ease off slowly into the praise and massage and instead just grab and release him quickly, he may become fearful of your hands. He may even think you are playing a game of "you nip at me and I'll nip back."

Some Don'ts for Using the Scruff Grip

- **Don't** use the scruff grip on dogs that have aggressive tendencies—dogs that snap, growl, or bite; dogs that are very nervous, hand- or collar-shy, or have been abused. If you have an aggressive, shy, or fearful dog, seek professional help.

- **Don't** violently shake your dog around when you have him in the scruff grip. All you have to do is grip, glare, and lecture. If you need further emphasis, gently shake the skin only.

- **Don't** pin your dog to the floor on his back—it will only panic him. You can combine the scruff grip with a right-side-up push to the floor if he has just done something near the floor, such as grabbing your ankle or pant leg.

- **Don't** grip your dog anywhere near his throat. This will panic him—and rightly so—and he may get aggressive. Make sure to grip him on the back of his neck only.

- **Don't** grab your dog's ears; they are very sensitive.

- **Don't** pull so hard on his neck that you pull his throat tight. If you do so he will feel that you are choking him and will panic—again, rightly so.

- **Don't** stab your dog with long fingernails. Sharp nails can cut his sensitive skin and cause your dog to react with pain and fear. He may even become hostile if he feels he's gotten "bitten" by you. Make sure your nails are short while your dog is growing up and needs hands-on handling, or avoid using this method.

Remember, the goal here is not to hurt your dog, but to let him know, on your terms, that his current behavior is unacceptable to you.

THE SHAKER CAN

Another useful tool, the shaker can, is a homemade device that gives you an effective hands-off method of interrupting your dog and getting her attention when she is misbehaving.

You can make a shaker can by dropping eight to ten small pebbles into an empty soda can; the heavier the pebbles, the deeper the tone will be. Flip the pop top back over the opening, squish the sides a bit for easy identification, and you have a very useful training tool.

(Don't put pennies in the can; they make a higher sound that isn't as startling.)

When you shake the can quickly, it makes a loud, startling sound, somewhat like a growl. When your dog hears the can growling, she will stop whatever she was doing. The shaker can is a useful backup to your voice, especially if you have trouble sounding stern enough.

The first time you use the can on your dog, be dramatic, so she can't help but notice what's happening, but if you have a sensitive dog, don't scare the daylights out of her by rattling the can too energetically. A series of quieter shakes may be all you need. And keep in mind that some dogs will just be plain terrified of this device. If this is the case, get rid of the can and use the other tools instead.

When you shake the can, reprimand your dog verbally as well. Use whatever words the situation calls for: "Leave it," "No," or "Off." After your dog has stopped misbehaving, praise her and guide her into more acceptable behavior such as a sit-stay, and praise her for that as well. Then do a calming massage, to make her feel appreciated.

Keep the shaker can well out of reach of your dog and your children. Don't let the pebbles rattle around between uses. Carry the can around carefully so the pebbles don't make any noise. If your dog hears the can rattle now and again, she'll become desensitized to the sound and may end up playing with it.

If necessary, use six or more cans and stash them all over the house. One on the counter for food thieving, one stuffed behind the couch cushions for crash landings in your lap, one outside the front door for attempts to bolt outside, one inside the front door for jumping up, one in the car for leaping around wildly, one in the playroom for tackling the kids, and so on. You get the idea.

THE SPRAY BOTTLE

A spray bottle—the type used for misting plants—is a quiet, hands-off way of interrupting your dog when he's misbehaving. Get a bottle that has a spray setting in addition to the mist and stream settings; it is the spray that you will be using. Choose a bottle small enough to fit in your coat pocket. Fill it with tap water and *test the settings* before using it on your dog.

Spray your dog when he is misbehaving—or when he is just about to. Hold the bottle far enough away from your dog's head so when you spray him, you spray his whole head. The sooner your spritz him, the better. At the moment you spritz your dog, speak firmly to him, saying, "Leave it!" or "Off!" or "No!"—whatever is appropriate for the behavior. Once your dog has stopped the behavior, praise him, then have him sit and stay, and do a calming massage to settle him down. You can use the spray bottle in conjunction with the leash snap. The spray bottle is especially useful for stopping unwanted barking. If you have a dog with aggressive tendencies, for which you should get professional help, the spray bottle is a hands-off, humbling, startling, and attention-getting correction.

Because it is silent, the spray bottle is useful when you don't want to scare others, such as children and cats. If you spray your dog for lunging at your cat, only your dog will be startled.

As great a tool as the spray bottle is, sometimes it's not the best way to go. Some dogs think the spray is fun. Others just ignore it. In hot weather, your dog may actually enjoy the cooling effect. Also, if you have a Lhasa or an Old English sheepdog, the hair over the dog's eyes will prevent him from noticing the spritz of water. For very hairy dogs, use the shaker can instead, or trim the hair back from the dog's eyes.

Part Two

Dog

Problems

from A to Z

USING THE A-TO-Z ENTRIES

E ach A-to-Z entry has five parts:

1. *Problem:* This section simply states and identifies the unwanted behavior.

2. *Why your dog is doing this:* This section explains the situation from your dog's point of view. Since everything your dog does is perfectly natural from his perspective, once you understand the logic of your dog's actions, you will find it easier to help him.

3. *What to say and do:* This section gives you detailed instructions on how to correct your dog at the instant the misbehavior occurs. Long-term suggestions are then provided for creating an environment conducive to good habits.

4. *Why this works:* This section explains exactly why your dog will respond to your disciplinary actions.

5. *Prevention:* This section explains what you can do to prevent this problem from happening again.

If your dog has so many bad habits that you don't know where to start, begin by implementing the prevention suggestions. At the same time, start your dog on a structured obedience-training program and twenty minutes a day of calming massage sessions. Give yourself a week or so to pick out one or two problems that are the least overwhelming and work on those first. Success breeds confidence, so start easy.

A WORD ABOUT CORRECTIONS

I n training you will often have to correct your dog, so you need to know that there are three parts to every correction. First, interrupt your dog's unwanted behavior; second, guide her into the correct behavior; and third, praise her for cooperating.

A correction can be very simple: "Gypsy, off the couch" (interruption); "Here's your bed" (guidance); "Good girl" (praise). If your dog needs extra encouragement, thank her for giving you her attention after the interruption.

Always use the mildest possible method of interrupting your dog and getting her attention. Remember, if you are too harsh with her, you will frighten her. This could make a sensitive dog timid, or it could cause your dog to panic and react aggressively. Never use a training session as an excuse to overwhelm or intimidate your dog. Always teach her in a gentle and loving way.

A NOTE ABOUT WORKING WITH YOUNG PUPPIES

M ost of the instructions in the A-to-Z section of this book are designed for dogs older than six months. Younger puppies must be treated even more gently and positively, and possibly with different methods. Some of the correctional techniques outlined here will work fine for young pups of a certain temperament, but only in the mildest of forms (some of the entries have specific puppy instructions). If you have a young puppy, concentrate more on following the suggestions in the "Prevention" sections than on the correctional measures.

THE A-TO-Z ENTRIES

ABUSED DOG

Problem: I think my dog has been abused. If I raise my voice, she crouches down, frightened. Whenever I reach out to pet her, she cowers.

Why your dog is doing this: If your dog has been abused, she is afraid of being hurt again and is afraid of people. Her trust has been weakened, and when she hears loud voices or sees hands, feet, or objects coming at her, she cringes, expecting to be hit or kicked.

What to say and do: You need to restore your dog's trust in humans. Your handling of her must be consistently respectful and sensitive before she will begin to relax.

1. Always speak to your dog in a soothing voice before you reach out *slowly* to pet her. Tell her how sweet she is, and that you are not going to hurt her.

2. Slowly squat down to her level to make yourself smaller and less threatening. Take a deep breath to relax yourself, and pat your leg invitingly. Keep talking to her in a soothing voice.

3. Hold your hand out for her to sniff, keeping it under her chin. Never reach toward the top of her head, which will scare her. Let her sniff you. Then slowly stroke her throat or the side of her neck. Don't make any sudden moves and continue to talk in a sweet, soft voice. As she relaxes, slide your hand around to her chest and body. Keep your touch gentle and slow. This procedure should be followed every time you want to touch your dog.

4. If she's still jumpy and frightened, offer her some small treats, one at a time, with one hand while you get her accustomed to being touched with your other hand.

5. Always speak in your mildest voice tones when you need to correct her, and use very gentle hands to guide her into the correct behavior. Praise her the instant she starts to cooperate.

6. If you are yelling at another dog or a human, and she becomes frightened, immediately turn to her and switch your voice to sweet and reassuring tones, saying to her, "You're okay sweetie. You're good."

7. Spend at least twenty minutes a day giving your dog a calming massage. This will help remove the fear as well as the memories that go with it. Start gently and use a lot of slow strokes, from behind her eyes down over her ears and the rest of her body. Find the areas where she enjoys being touched and work those first.

8. Find some quiet games that she enjoys and play with her. Let her explore in the park on a long line so she can relax her body. Don't make any sudden movements that might spook her.

9. If possible, find her a confident and outgoing doggy friend to spend time with. This will help her relax and become more trusting.

10. Obedience training is a confidence builder when done sensitively and with lots of praise and patience. Keep your hand movements slow and sensitive, and speak to her continually in an encouraging, praising tone.

Why this works: If you are consistent and sensitive and gentle in your communication and handling of your dog, she will learn to trust you.

Prevention: Be aware how your every move and sound affects your dog. Always use the mildest voice possible to get the message across, praising her instantly when she cooperates. Don't let anyone tease your dog, and be sure to instruct others in how to make friends with her and pet her. Never hit her, corner her, or grab at her, and don't overcorrect her. Feed her a natural, additive-free diet, to help her nervous system.

WARNING: If your dog is so frightened that she growls or snaps at you or anyone else, get professional help.

See also:
Fear of certain objects
Nervousness
Hand-shyness
Shyness

AFRAID TO BE ALONE

Problem: My dog wants to be with me all the time. Whenever I leave her alone, even for a little while, she whines, barks, chews, scratches on the door, and sometimes relieves herself.

Why your dog is doing this: Because dogs are pack animals and need to live in family groups, they may feel insecure when left alone. You are her family and her security, and when you leave she feels abandoned and panics. Anxiety causes her to chew nervously and can upset her stomach. She barks and whines in the hope of helping you find your way back to her.

What to say and do:

1. Set up a place where you can confine her. This can be a spacious wire exercise pen or a room with a baby gate across the open doorway. Never shut your dog up behind a closed door. Her space should ideally be in or adjacent to an area where you spend a lot of time, such as your family room or kitchen. Get her a cozy bed, some toys, and a water bowl. Dogproof the area so there is nothing that can hurt her or that she can destroy. Spend at least twenty minutes a day in her special place giving her a calming massage. Get her used to being in her space, but don't confine her alone in it yet.

2. Practice obedience training indoors, especially in her space, until she is capable of doing fifteen- to twenty-minute down-stays at the end of a 6-foot leash, both on her bed and on the floor. Then, still in her space, begin to practice off-leash.

3. When she's comfortable in her space, practice the down-stay while you stand outside of her space with a baby gate set up as a barrier. Pass the leash over the gate. Leave her for only three minutes to start; then return and praise her. Repeat this several times, leaving her alone slightly longer each time; praise her calmly and quietly when you return.

4. Take the leash off and leave the room. Tell her firmly but kindly, "You stay in your room." Now walk away, but remain in sight. If she acts up, rush back and tell her firmly, "You stop that. You stay in your room." If she ignores you, use the shaker can, spray bottle, or scruff shake. Then walk away immediately.

5. If she remains calm for five minutes, return to her, calmly praising her as you approach. Stroke her slowly and then leave again. In a cautioning voice say, "You stay in your room." Gradually increase the amount of time she can handle being alone, first with you in sight, then with you out of sight but still at home.

6. When you begin to see some improvement, leave the house and follow the same procedure. Reprimand her verbally if she acts up. Next, try some mock departures. Gather up your car keys and coat and leave the house. Walk away noisily, or drive a short distance and park down the street. Then sneak back to your house and spy on her, dashing in to correct her, if necessary.

7. When you return from a real outing, sneak up to your house to see if she's barking. If so, correct her. Then leave again, and return only after she's been quiet for several minutes.

Why this works: Obedience training builds confidence, encourages self-control, and teaches your dog to respect you and take you seriously. Calming massages will help relax her and remove the tension from her body. By doing these things with her in her special place, you help her to feel safe.

Prevention: It is important to teach young dogs to accept being alone, whether in a crate, a yard, an exercise pen, or a special place behind a baby gate. Once she is crate-trained, your dog will view her crate as a secure, safe den, and you can crate her for short periods if she is not trustworthy loose in the house. If you would like to crate-train her, your first step is to make the crate her cozy bed.

Give your dog plenty of exercise every day, especially if you must leave her alone. If you have to be gone long hours, see about a dog-walking service or schedule some doggy playmates to keep her entertained.

Keep your hellos and good-byes unemotional. This will help your dog see that your comings and goings aren't such a big deal. If she is acting up, don't give her sympathy; correct her and leave her immediately.

See also:
Crate training

BABIES, OVEREXUBERANCE TOWARD

Problem: My dog just loves my new baby and is always jumping up to lick him. I'm concerned she might accidentally hurt him.

Why your dog is doing this: Your dog is fascinated with the baby, and because the baby is small and helpless, your dog finds him an easy target for affection and licking. She may have a maternal instinct, or she could see the baby as a new toy.

What to say and do:

1. The instant your dog begins to get excited around your baby, interrupt her with a very firm verbal correction. If necessary, use the shaker can (if it doesn't bother the baby), the spray bottle, the scruff grip, or a leash snap.

2. As soon as your dog stops and gives you her attention, have her sit and stay; then calm her down with slow hands and a neck massage. Talk kindly to her and explain that she has to be gentle around the baby. When she's calm, let her sniff the baby and even give him a lick or two.

3. Watch your dog closely. If she starts to become too exuberant, correct her again; alternate between correction and calming massage as needed. After she sniffs or licks the baby, you can let her remain around you only as long as she's calm. If she's too bouncy, send her away or put her in a down-stay.

4. Practice obedience commands on a daily basis, and do so in the presence of your baby.

Why this works: Let your dog know that you will not tolerate wild enthusiasm around your baby. Following your corrections with an obedience command will teach her to control herself. A massage will calm her down.

Prevention: Give your dog plenty of exercise, so she can work off her excess energy somewhere other than on the baby. If time is short, find a dog walker or schedule regular visits with a doggy playmate.

Practice the obedience commands with your dog in the house on a daily basis and give her occasional commands throughout the day. Let her remain nearby as you take care of your baby, but keep her under control. Make sure that she sits and stays before you pet her, especially if you are holding the baby.

Spend some quality time alone with your dog every day, in play, training, quiet time, and massage.

WARNING: *Never leave your dog alone with your baby.* An over-enthusiastic dog might get carried away and mouth (chew on) the baby. If you have any doubts about your dog's intentions, get professional help.

See also:
Excitable behavior
Playing too exuberantly with kids

Babies, Resentment of

Problem: My dog hasn't been the same since I brought home my new baby. He mopes around all the time, bugs me for attention, and continually gets into trouble.

Why your dog is doing this: Your dog feels left out because he probably hasn't been getting as much attention and exercise as he did before the baby arrived. He doesn't feel like a member of the family pack anymore, and the insecurity that results can make him resentful and jealous of your baby. Just like some children, your dog finds that his misbehavior gets your attention, and he repeats it just to get noticed.

What to say and do:

1. You need to reassure your dog that he's still a beloved member of the family. He needs to be included in your daily routine, spend quality time with you, and find the baby fun to have around.

2. Include the dog in your daily activities by talking to him happily about the baby: "Rex, let's go see why the baby is crying. Come on, boy!" Give him a pat on the head as you invite him to go with you to attend to the baby.

3. Sit on the floor or in a low chair holding your baby, and invite your dog to come up and say hello; "Rex, come and say hi to the baby. Good boy, say hi!" Let him give the baby a sniff and a lick or two if he wants to or if he's curious. Stroke your dog and your baby, talking sweetly and happily.

4. If your dog likes to retrieve, toss a toy for him while you hold your baby. Talk happily as you play, and let your dog see that the baby can be fun to be around.

5. Give your dog a calming message with one hand while you hold your baby with the other. (This is where three hands would be helpful!)

Why this works: Finding little ways to keep your dog amused and to include him in your daily life will help him feel that he is still a welcome member of your family. Speaking happily to him when he is around the baby will help him view the baby as a pleasant companion rather than a competitor. Massage will relax him and make him feel loved.

Prevention: Make sure your dog continues to do the things he enjoyed doing before the baby arrived. Review his obedience training. Teach him a few new commands, if you wish. Obedience sessions are a form of quality time, so practice a little bit every day. (A couple of upbeat five-minute sessions will help a lot.) Daily exercise will lift his spirits. If time is short, try to find a doggy playmate or a dog walker.

Prepare your dog for the baby's arrival by making any necessary changes in the dog's routine—like no longer sleeping on the bed, for instance, before your baby comes home. Careful preparation will keep your dog from viewing the baby as an intruder who has disrupted his life.

WARNING: If your dog growls or snaps at your baby, get professional help immediately. *Never leave the dog alone with the baby.*

See also:
Depression

Babies: Toddlers

Problem: My toddler follows my dog everywhere. The dog really loves the baby, but I can see that her patience is beginning to run out. She even snapped at him a couple of times.

Why your dog is doing this: The only way your dog can express her impatience is to snap. This is the same treatment she would give an obnoxious puppy. This behavior, while unsettling, is perfectly natural, since a dog cannot just open her mouth and say "Leave me alone."

What to say and do:

WARNING: If your dog is growling or snapping at your child, *get professional help.*

1. Monitor all interactions between your dog and your child. Teach your toddler how to stroke the dog gently. Talk happily to your dog and scratch her favorite places with your free hand. Keep the baby's hello sessions short and pleasant and end them while your dog is still enjoying herself.

2. If your toddler comes over while you are petting your dog, say very happily to the dog, "What a good girl you are! Here comes the baby. Let's say hi to the baby. Good girl!" Keep the hello brief and cheerful. Scoop up the baby and either continue to pet your dog or encourage her to leave with lots of praise.

3. If your dog growls or snaps at your toddler, correct her firmly: "No! Shame on you." If necessary, use the spray bottle or scruff grip on her. Calm the dog with a massage, and then encourage her to leave, and praise her for going.

4. If your dog likes to retrieve, play with her while you hold the baby. As soon as your child is old enough, help him throw a toy for the dog.

Why this works: Monitoring all interactions will ensure that your dog does not get poked, prodded, rolled on, tweaked, or cornered. When your dog finds your child's touch pleasant and sees that he is fun to be around, she'll be more likely to welcome him.

Correcting her instantly and firmly for being intolerant will let her know that you will not stand for that behavior, and calming her afterward will help her relax.

Prevention: Teach your child not to chase, follow, tease, or corner your dog and not to disturb the dog when she's resting.

Every time your child touches your dog, be there to hold and guide your child's hand. This will prevent any accidental grabbing or poking. No matter how patient she is, any dog's patience can run out, and any dog can bite. Remember to protect the dog from the child and the child from the dog.

Teach or review your dog's obedience training daily. This will serve as quality time and will remind her of her position in your household.

Give your dog a cozy retreat that your toddler can't get to where she can rest undisturbed. Put a crate or exercise pen in your family room, or partition off a porch or spare room with a baby gate so your dog can see you and not feel isolated. When you can't be there to supervise dog and child, separate them.

Encourage your dog to escape from your child's advances. When your baby wanders over to your dog, tell her, "Look out, here comes the baby! Up you go. Go away." Sound upbeat and positive, and praise her for leaving. If possible, provide an escape route and teach your dog to use it. This could be a barrier your dog can jump over or a dog door for a small dog to slip through into a safe haven.

WARNING: *Never leave your dog and toddler alone together unattended, even for short periods.*

See also:
Crate training
Snapping at your children

BARKING AT GUESTS

Problem: Whenever someone comes to the door, my dog gets very excited and won't stop barking.

Why your dog is doing this: It's natural for your dog to bark when someone enters her territory. She is merely protecting you, your home, and your possessions.

What to say and do:

1. Arrange visits from friends so you and your dog can practice greeting visitors. When the doorbell rings and your dog starts barking, say to her, "Who's there? Who is it? Good girl, let's go see!" Call out to the visitor, "Who there?" Speak in a worried, whispering tone. This lets your dog know that you want a few alarm barks.

2. If you know the visitor, switch your voice to a happy, friendly tone, saying, "It's okay. It's just Sally! Let's say hello to Sally," and chatter away happily. Hold your dog by the collar, open the door, and greet your friend with a handshake or hug so your dog can see you making friendly contact. If your dog stops barking and greets your friend, as many dogs will do at this point, fine. If she's very exuberant, have her sit before she gets petted.

3. If your dog doesn't stop barking, give her a sharp yank on the collar and say firmly, "Quiet. That's enough barking. It's okay." Make her sit and calm her with massage and praise such as "Good sit, good girl to be quiet." Repeat the correction sequence if necessary, using the spray bottle or shaker can, if necessary. When she is calm, encourage her to say hello to your guest.

4. If you don't know the visitor and you want your dog to continue to bark, don't switch to the happy tone. Keep your voice more formal and guarded when speaking to the visitor and ignore your dog's barking. After your guest leaves, praise your dog.

Why this works: Your dog is barking because an outsider has entered her territory. When you make that person familiar to your dog she will have no reason to keep barking.

Prevention: Practice this exercise many times with a variety of helpers.

If necessary, keep a leash on your dog when you are expecting visitors so she will be easier to get hold of and control. Practice her obedience commands around the front door.

Spend twenty minutes a day giving her a calming massage in a distraction-free, quiet place. Socialize her in public or enroll her in an obedience class where she will meet lots of people in a controlled setting.

See also:
Abused dog
Shyness

BARKING AT NEIGHBORS

Problem: My dog barks at the neighbors whenever he sees them in their yard.

Why your dog is doing this: Your dog is barking at the neighbors because they are strangers to him.

What to say and do:

1. Introduce your dog to your neighbors on common ground between the two properties. If your dog is apprehensive, provide your neighbors with some treats to offer him.

2. Next, ask your neighbors to come into your backyard and stay for a while. Have them call your dog, use his name often, offer him treats, pet him, and maybe play a game of fetch.

3. Now it's time for your neighbors to go back into their own yard with treats they can offer your dog through the fence (a knothole will do). They need to talk happily to your dog, use his name, and feed him yummy treats.

4. Go indoors, leaving your dog alone in the yard with the neighbors still visiting with him through the fence. If your dog is quiet and calm, ask your neighbors to go in and out of their house several times, call happily to your dog each time they reenter their yard, and give him a treat. Repeat this sequence from step one, if necessary, several times over several days.

5. If you suspect that your dog is being teased or mistreated by a neighbor's child, discuss the situation with the parents, who may be unaware of the problem. And, most important, *do not leave your dog unattended in the yard* until this problem has been resolved.

Why this works: Your dog barks at your neighbors because they are strangers. Letting your dog meet your neighbors gives him a chance to make friends with them, and he will remember who they are, even after they return to their own yard.

Prevention: Socialize your dog from a young age. Introduce him to new people and situations. Take him for walks around your neighborhood and for car rides. Have visitors give your dog treats or play with him.

Make sure your dog has a comfortable doghouse and toys to keep him busy. Take care that he does not spend too much time alone in the yard.

When your neighbors are in their backyard, greet them happily so your dog sees that you are not threatened by them.

BARKING AT OTHER DOGS

Problem: Whenever my dog sees another dog, she barks wildly and ignores my demands for silence.

Why your dog is doing this: It's a great event for your dog to see another dog. She barks to attract attention to herself and to express her happiness at finding a potential playmate. On the other hand, if she is overly frustrated by not having met many other dogs, she could be barking as an aggressive challenge.

What to say and do:

1. The instant your dog sees another dog (even a block away) and perks up her ears, talk happily and sweetly to her: "Look, Samantha, there's a pretty dog down the street." Keep her leash slack and let her know you aren't upset or tense.

2. If she starts to bark, instantly snap the leash sharply a couple of times and use the spray bottle. Verbally correct her strongly, saying, "Leave it! Quiet! No barking!" Then have her sit. Praise her and talk to her sweetly and happily while you do some calming massage on her neck. Be ready to correct her immediately should she resume barking. If she is too excited to stop barking or sit still, put her through a snappy obedience drill with lots of heeling and sits. Keep her busy having to focus on you.

3. If you have your dog on-leash and another dog comes near her, speak happily to your dog, casually stand out of the way, and keep her leash slack so as not to transmit tension to your dog. Let the dogs sniff each other while you keep the leash from getting tangled. Don't show any fear or you might trigger a fight.

4. If your dog is off-leash and meets another dog, stand back or even walk away and leave them alone. After the dogs have checked each other out, invite your dog along casually as you walk away.

Why this works: This approach lets your dog see that you think other dogs are fun. Correcting your dog instantly for barking keeps her from getting too worked up. Following the correction with the sit command gives her something she can to do control herself, please you, and get praised for. The calming work helps her to relax. You're sending her a message that it's bad to bark, good to stop, and good to sit and calm down.

Prevention: Spend twenty minutes per day in calming sessions in a quiet place. Obedience-train your dog and practice thirty minutes per day, indoors at first and then in front of your home.

If you're sure she's not a fighter or a roamer, socialize your dog as much as possible off-leash in safe areas. Often, informal doggy play groups form in local parks. Enlist the aid of a friend with a calm dog who will "appear" down the block when you are out for a walk. Practice the training routine while your friend's dog is in the distance. Then get closer as your dog learns to behave herself.

If you are not satisfied with training her on your own, enroll your dog in an obedience class, so she can get used to being around other dogs in a controlled setting.

If you have a male dog, neutering will help reduce his aggressive tendencies.

BARKING AT STRANGERS

Problem: Whenever my dog sees a stranger, she barks. She's not mean, but she scares people.

Why your dog is doing this: Your dog is warning you that a stranger is too close for comfort and that she feels both threatened and protective.

What to say and do:

1. The instant she alerts to someone (as soon as her ears go up), reassure her in a happy, relaxed voice: "It's okay, sweetie. You don't have to bark."

2. If this doesn't work, give her a firm verbal correction, and be ready to use the shaker can, spray bottle, scruff grip, or leash snap.

Then have her sit. Praise her, and calm her with massage. Alternate between the correction and the calm praise as needed.

3. If the stranger is someone you want her to meet, say hello to the person in a happy voice. Let her sniff him while he gives her some treats that you have provided. Don't rush your dog into saying hello or being petted, and don't let the stranger make any sudden moves.

4. If you want your dog to bark at this stranger because he seems threatening to you, encourage her to bark by sounding *worried*. Speak softly and urgently: "Who is it? Who's there? Watch him!" Praise her for barking: "Good girl!" When you want her to quit, tell her, "That's enough. Thank you. Quiet now."

Why this works: Your dog is barking at strangers because they are unfamiliar to her. By giving her clear feedback, you are letting her know whether you want her to bark at them or not. Your correction stops her barking; your command to sit gives her something acceptable to do with her body; your massage helps her to calm down; and your friendliness helps her to be friendly.

Prevention: When you dog first alerts you to someone, even if the person is a block away, start talking in a reassuring voice and distract her with some simple obedience commands to get her attention back to you.

Obedience training, especially in a group class, will socialize your dog and will teach her to pay attention to you even though there are lots of distractions. Practice the obedience commands indoors, on the street, at the park, and anywhere else you take her.

Spend twenty minutes a day doing a calm massage session. This will help her to settle down more quickly when she's in her barking mode.

BARKING FOR ATTENTION

Problem: When my dog wants my attention, she barks at me. She always barks when I'm on the telephone.

Why your dog is doing this: She would like some of the attention you are giving the telephone and she knows that if she barks you will acknowledge her in some way.

What to say and do:

1. Keep a short leash on her that she can drag around the house while you are with her. Make sure the end doesn't get caught on anything. When she begins to bark, grab the leash, give her a leash snap correction, and tell her, "Quiet! No barking!" If that proves ineffective, use the spray bottle or shaker can.

2. When she quiets down tell her, "Good to be quiet," have her sit and stay, and praise her for doing so. If necessary, help her to settle down with a calming massage. If she starts barking again, repeat the correction.

Why this works: Leaving a short leash on your dog allows you to correct her as soon as she starts barking. She finds out quickly that you won't tolerate such behavior.

Prevention: Make sure your dog gets some quality attention from you every day. Always be sure to provide her with toys to play with and gnaw on.

Obedience training, in addition to providing quality time, will teach her to take you seriously. Use the down-stay to settle her; it is hard for dogs to bark while they are lying down. Never reward your dog with attention or a treat just to shut her up. If she is tiny, don't pick her up to quiet her.

If your dog is crate-trained, you can put her in her crate during those times when you simply can't be with her. But don't let the crate become a substitute for training her not to bark other times.

See also:
    Crate training

BARKING IN THE CAR

Problem: My dog barks and leaps about wildly when she's in the car, whether we're driving or parked. Not only is it a hassle to take her anywhere, but her behavior could cause me to have an accident.

Why your dog is doing this: Your dog is excited by everything new, and she wants everyone to notice her. She is also guarding the car from everything and everyone outside because she has claimed it as her territory.

What to say and do:

1. Sit with your dog in your car while remaining parked on the street. Have a leash attached to her choke chain, and have the spray bottle and shaker can handy in case she starts barking or leaping about wildly. Give her a calming massage on her neck and speak sweetly to her.

2. If she perks up her ears or starts barking, tell her, "You silly dog, you don't have to bark at that. Be quiet." Sound relaxed and reassuring, to show her you are not worried. If she stops barking, fine—praise her and resume her neck massage.

3. If she ignores your reassurance, immediately say, "Quiet! No barking!" and at the same time use the leash snap. You can add the shaker can or spray bottle, whichever you prefer, if necessary. Command her to sit, praise her for being quiet, and resume the neck massage. Alternate between the firm correction, the sit command, and calm massage or praise, as needed. Practice this in the car with her for as many days as it takes.

4. Stand outside the car and be ready to correct her for unwanted barking. The spray bottle is effective through a partially open window.

5. Get a helper for this part of the lesson. (It is dangerous to drive and try to train your dog at the same time.) Have your helper drive you around while you sit with your dog in the back seat and continue the training. While your helper drives around, practice until the dog is calm.

6. Now try a solo trip. If your dog starts barking, correct her instantly with the spray bottle and tell her, "Quiet," and "Sit," in a firm tone of voice, and be careful; remember you are driving. If she starts to get out of hand, pull over and correct her when the car has stopped. If you have her on a leash, be careful that it doesn't get tangled in anything.

Why this works: By teaching your dog while your car is parked, you are able to focus entirely on her, correcting her the instant she acts up. Having a helper drive you around allows you the same opportunity to focus on her while the car is moving. Because she will be getting corrected instantly, she will learn that you will not tolerate misbehavior in the car.

Prevention: Practice the obedience lessons before you get in the car. This will remind her that you are in control before she even gets into the car. If she is an excessive barker at other times—in the house, in the yard, or on walks, for example—work on correcting that particular behavior.

Try to anticipate when she will bark by watching her ears closely. When she perks them up, alert to something, correct her *before* she begins to bark. It is also helpful to drive her around the neighborhood, so she can get used to things outside the car.

BARKING IN THE HOUSE WHEN ALONE

Problem: My dog barks or howls when she's alone in my house.

Why your dog is doing this: Since dogs are pack animals, your dog feels abandoned and insecure when you leave her alone. A dog lost in the wilderness will instinctively howl in order to guide her packmates back to her. When she's home alone, she cries in the hope of bringing you back.

What to say and do:

1. If your dog barks excessively when you are home, you must correct that problem before teaching her to be quiet when you are gone. Go to the next entry, "Barking in the house when you're home," and return to this section later on.

2. When your dog is ready for this lesson, pretend to leave, taking your coat and car keys. Take the shaker can with you. Leave your door unlocked so you are set up for a quick surprise return. Sneak back, position yourself outside the door, and wait.

3. As soon as your dog begins to bark, dash back inside, shake the can rapidly at her, and reprimand her strongly as you come through the door: "Quiet! Shame on you—no barking. Be quiet." Leave as quickly as you entered. Now—and this is the hardest part—do not use any kind words, no matter how crushed your dog looks.

4. Station yourself outside again and wait. If your dog is quiet for five minutes, reenter, saying kindly as you open the door, "What a good dog to be so quiet! Thank you!" and stroke her calmly. Switch your voice to a warning tone, say, "Stay quiet. You be good," and leave.

5. When you see progress, leave her alone for ten minutes, then fifteen minutes, then thirty minutes. Build up to an hour or two.

6. When you actually have to go somewhere, allow extra time to sneak back inside and surprise your dog if necessary. When you return, park a block away and sneak up to your house, listening for your dog. Correct the barking, if necessary, and go back outside. Make your dog wait quietly inside before you return to her.

Why this works: Correcting your dog in the act of barking is the only way she will learn not to bark. When she barks to bring back her beloved human and you barge back into the house angry, she will think twice about barking.

Prevention: Leave the radio on a soothing station to help mask the sounds outside. Give your dog plenty of exercise so she'll be tired when you leave, and make certain she has a cozy bed and toys to play with and chew on.

Make your comings and goings low-key.

Practice obedience training indoors so your dog will associate control and confidence with being inside. If you have time, put her through a short drill just before you leave the house.

If you must be gone for long hours, try to give your dog access to a fenced yard, hire a dog walker to come and exercise her during the day, or find a doggy day care situation for her. Let your neighbors know that you are working on the barking problem and ask them to give you progress reports.

If these tactics prove unsuccessful, you must teach your dog to accept being separated from you while both of you are in the house.

See also:
Afraid to be alone
Crate training

BARKING IN THE HOUSE WHEN YOU'RE HOME

Problem: My dog barks frantically at every little thing, even when I'm home. She loves to stand at the window or out on the deck and warn away imaginary monsters.

Why your dog is doing this: Your dog needs to be taught when it's okay to bark and when it's not okay, especially if she's young. If she feels threatened, she'll bark out of insecurity. If she's bored, she'll bark to entertain herself.

What to say and do:

1. Follow your dog and find out what is upsetting her. Ask her, "What is it? Who's there?" Sound worried. If it is something you want her to bark at, encourage her. When it's time for her to stop, switch your voice to one of relaxed praise. "Good dog!" Then have her sit, and calm her with a slow massage.

2. If you find that there's nothing to worry about, tell your dog happily, "It's okay. Don't worry." If she quiets down, praise her calmly, and slowly massage her.

3. If she ignores you and continues to bark, reprimand her firmly: "Quiet! No Barking!" Also use the scruff grip, shaker can, or spray bottle, if necessary. If you have a leash on her, do a leash snap. Then make her sit and calm her with massage. Alternate between firm correction and calm praise and massage as needed.

Why this works: By making yourself part of the process, you are letting her know that you respect and appreciate her service as watchdog. If you sound worried at first and then switch to a relaxed voice, your dog will follow your lead.

The daily play and exercise will reduce your dog's energy level, and tired dogs are less inclined to bark at everything.

If you are consistent in your guidance—bad to bark, good to sit, good to calm down under my hands—you will help her learn what is expected of her.

Prevention: Anticipate when your dog is going to bark, and warn her not to. The instant she perks her ears up, caution her and correct her if necessary. When she is quiet, praise her calmly and warmly.

Spend a minimum of twenty minutes a day practicing her obedience training. This will help her to take you seriously when you correct her for barking. If certain things inevitably set her off, practice with her while she is distracted. Put her in a down-stay, which makes it harder for her to bark.

Make sure your dog gets plenty of exercise every day. Make sure she is not spending too much time indoors alone. Provide her with toys and things to gnaw on; this will give her mouth something to do other than bark. Give her a cozy bed in the house or crate-train her.

See also:
Crate training

BARKING IN THE YARD AT NIGHT

Problem: My dog barks on and off all night. It's driving my neighbors crazy.

Why your dog is doing this: Your dog could be barking for one or all of the following reasons: loneliness, insecurity, protectiveness, boredom, frustration, or excess energy.

What to say and do:

1. The simplest solution, and one your dog will appreciate enormously, is to bring him indoors at night. If your dog spends all day in the yard, away from you, why not let him sleep in your room at night so he can have some "people time"? Even though you're asleep, this still counts as quality time.

2. If at first you cannot have him in your room or loose in the house, give him access (via a dog door) to a cozy, sectioned-off bed area inside your house, basement, porch, or garage, provided it doesn't smell of gas and oil. Be very careful to remove any poisons such as antifreeze and slug bait. Also remove all sharp tools and other objects that could injure your dog. Leave a radio on to mask some of the outside sounds.

3. Once he is used to his inside sleeping area, you can confine him there all night by closing off the dog door. Be sure he has relieved himself outside first. Provide him with toys and things to gnaw on, such as safe rawhide chews. Crate training is an alternative that will allow him to be confined indoors, yet be in your room with you.

4. When he does bark in the evenings, go outside and find out what's troubling him. If it is something you want him to bark at, ask him, "Who is it? Who's there?" Praise him for barking. When you want him to stop, reassure him, "It's okay. That's enough barking." If he doesn't stop, correct him firmly and, if necessary, use the spray bottle, shaker can, or scruff grip. Command him to sit, and calm him with massage.

5. If he's barking at something you don't want him to bark at, try stopping him by speaking in a ridiculing tone: "You silly dog, you don't need to bark at that." This shows him you're not worried about what he's barking at. If that doesn't work, be firmer. Correct him, and calm him.

6. If your dog barks excessively at other times as well, work on correcting that too. See appropriate Barking entries.

Why this works: If your dog is inside at night, he won't be outside barking. Training him in the yard, as well as calming him there, will help him see the yard as a place where there are rules and limits, and a place where he must take you seriously. Making yourself part of his watchdog process, by checking out what he's barking at and guiding him accordingly, gives him a clear lead to follow.

Prevention: Make sure your dog is not spending all his time isolated and imprisoned in the yard. Make the yard entertaining for him with toys, sandy digging areas, and rawhide bones to gnaw on. Spend twenty minutes a day, minimum, practicing his obedience lessons in the yard; give him calming massages there as well. It's important that he get enough exercise, as a tired dog is much less likely to bark. Bring him inside in the evenings and the entire night, if possible. He will be a much happier and safer dog, and he will make you happier, too.

See also:
Crate training

BARKING IN THE YARD WHEN ALONE

Problem: My dog barks when we leave him alone in the back-yard.

Why your dog is doing this: Your dog could be barking out of loneliness, fear, insecurity, frustration, or excess energy. Or he could be sending a warning to intruders, human or otherwise. If your dog spends too much time alone in the yard, he may become both unhappy and noisy.

What to say and do:

1. If your dog barks excessively when you are home, correct that problem first (see Barking in the yard when you're home).

2. If he continues to bark when you're away, orchestrate a fake departure. Slam the front door, but remain in the house, out of sight. Quietly observe your dog, and when he begins to bark, rush outside, firmly stating "No barking." Use the shaker can or spray bottle as startling backup to your firm voice. If you can easily grab him, use the scruff grip. Then quickly retreat back to the house. Remember, no kind words, and no praise.

3. Wait five to ten minutes. If he barks again, repeat your correction. Be dramatic. Let him know you aren't at all pleased, then go back inside. Again, no kind words and no praise. If he remains quiet for ten to fifteen minutes, return to him and praise him calmly as you approach: "What a good boy to be so quiet in the yard." Go back in the house, pretend to leave again, and repeat the whole process.

4. When you do need to leave, allow extra time to stage some mock departures and surprise reprimands. If necessary, drive your car down the block, walk back, and sneak into your house.

Why this works: Mock departures to set your dog up for a correction will allow you to catch him in the act of barking. When you combine this technique with obedience training and calming work in the yard, your dog will learn to take you seriously.

Prevention: Take your dog out for a morning romp before you leave. Tired dogs are less inclined to bark all day. If you must be gone for long hours, find a dog walker who can come by, or find a compatible dog for him to play with. There are probably several lonely dogs in your neighborhood who would love the company. A toy is also a good bet. Try leaving a mature beef knuckle or marrow bone for him to gnaw on. This will give him hours of entertainment.

Give your dog access to the house or basement by way of a dog door. If he's not trustworthy when he's loose in the house, section off a pen just inside the dog door. This will give him a quiet place to retreat to. Put some toys and bedding in this indoor pen, and leave a radio on to mask the outside noises.

If you can't give him access to the house, it will help immensely if his yard is at least adjacent to the back door. If he is isolated in a separate pen, he'll feel more abandoned and be more inclined to bark.

Create a fun habitat for your dog in the yard. A wading pool, a sandbox, and a collection of toys will give him something to do other than get bored and start barking. Give him a cozy doghouse to curl up in, too.

Let your dog sleep in your room at night. This counts as quality time with you even if you are asleep. It also helps your dog accept his yard time more easily.

See also:
Dog door, fear of

BARKING IN THE YARD WHEN YOU'RE HOME

Problem: When my dog is in the yard, he barks at every little thing, and sometimes at nothing, even when I'm home.

Why your dog is doing this: Your dog could be barking out of insecurity, boredom, frustration, excess energy, fear, loneliness, protectiveness, or just because it's fun.

What to say and do:

1. As soon as you hear your dog barking, find out what he's barking at. If it is something you want him to bark at, encourage him: "What is it? Who's there? Go check it out!" and speak in a soft, urgent tone. When you want him to stop, switch your voice to a happy, praising tone: "Good boy! Thank you! That's enough barking." If he quiets down, great. Have him sit and calm him with slow hands and massage.

2. If he continues to bark, correct him. If you have your hands on him, correct him with the scruff grip; look into his eyes and lecture him firmly. If he is on a leash, snap the leash a few times sharply enough to get his attention, and if necessary add the spray bottle or shaker can to the leash correction. Tell him, "Quiet! No barking!" Have him sit, give him a calming neck massage and speak sweetly to him. Alternate between correction and praise as needed. If he is at a distance from you, shake the can or throw it at him, or spray him with the spray bottle or a hose. Don't blast him with the full force of the hose, of course. Just startle him with a spray of water. Follow with praise when he quiets down.

3. The first few times he barks at something you want him to get used to, speak in a silly tone: "Sam what a silly dog you are. You don't have to bark at that." Sound unconcerned. If your dog sees how blasé you are, he may relax and stop barking. If he does, praise him and calm him with a massage.

4. If he continues to bark, correct him immediately and very firmly.

Why this works: By taking part in the watchdog process, you show your dog that you, his pack leader, are on top of things. Dealing consistently and quickly with unnecessary barking gives him a clearer understanding of what his job is and what pleases you. The massage helps him relax.

Prevention: Make sure your dog gets adequate exercise on a daily basis, since excess energy is a major contributor to excessive barking. Take him out for long walks and tiring romps in the park. Find doggy playmates for him and arrange playtimes.

Your dog should not spend his entire life alone in your yard. When you are home, let him come inside with you. Allow him to sleep inside at night, preferably in your room; this is especially important if you are away from him for long hours.

Try to determine what your dog is barking at. Is a cat walking on your fence? Are the neighborhood kids teasing your dog? See if the cause can be removed. If your dog can see through your fence, especially if it borders the street or an alley, try to patch up the holes.

Give your dog access to the house, basement, or porch via a dog door. If your dog cannot be trusted loose in the house, section off an area just inside the dog door, creating a pen. Put a cozy bed, some toys, and a water bowl in his area. Play the radio just loud enough to help mask some of the noises from outside. (Keep electrical cords well out of reach.)

If it is impossible to install a dog door, provide your dog with a cozy doghouse in the yard. Make sure he has toys to play with and things to gnaw on. This will give him something to do with his mouth other than bark. Give him a sandbox to dig in if he's into digging and a kid's wading pool if it's hot and he enjoys playing in water. Make the yard entertaining and interesting for him.

If his yard is not adjacent to your back door, and he is isolated from the house in a separate pen, he will feel more abandoned and be more inclined to bark. Give him a yard adjacent to a house door so he can sit on the porch and feel connected to the house and to you.

Spend at least thirty minutes a day in the yard with him, practicing his obedience lessons, giving him a soothing calming massage, and playing with him, and socialize your dog in your neighborhood, so he can become accustomed to all the noises and activity.

BARKING TO COME IN

Problem: Whenever I put my dog out in our fenced yard, he stands at the door and barks, howls, or whines incessantly.

Why your dog is doing this: Your dog would prefer to be inside with you. He barks in the hope that you will let him in. If he spends too much time in the yard, he might be feeling lonely and abandoned. Dog don't like to be banished to the yard without human company and they can suffer miserably and pine for companionship.

What to say and do:

1. Don't let your dog in when he is barking. Instead, surprise him with an angry word.

2. Open the door abruptly and bump him gently with it. Tell him, "Quiet, no barking! You be quiet!" and point an angry finger at him. Close the door immediately and wait quietly inside.

3. If the verbal corrections and door bump aren't working after several tries, step outside and use the shaker can, spray bottle, or scruff grip. Always correct him verbally as well and return quickly inside. Be sure to make eye contact when you correct your dog.

4. If he stays quiet for five minutes, open the door slowly, saying calmly, "Good boy, good to be so quiet." Give him a slow stroke or two and go back inside, warning him as you leave, "Now be quiet. No barking."

5. Increase the amount of time your dog can handle being outside and quiet. Be consistent and correct him whenever he begins to bark. Visit with him calmly after he's been quiet for a while. Then let him in.

Why this works: Correcting your dog while he is barking lets him know that barking annoys you. Letting him in when he is quiet teaches him that he'll be rewarded for his silence.

Prevention: Make sure your dog doesn't spend too much time all alone in the yard. If he's outside while you are at work, bring him in as soon as you get home and let him spend the afternoon and evening with you. Ideally, let him sleep in your room at night.

Make sure he has a comfortable doghouse in his yard and an area in the shade, as well as a big bowl of water. Provide toys for him to play with and gnaw on. A sandbox for digging and a wading pool in the summer will keep him entertained. Spend time with him in the yard. Practice obedience exercises, play, and read while he snoozes by your side.

Don't teach your dog to bark when he wants to come in. Be aware of his needs but let him in when you want to.

See also:
Afraid to be alone
Dog door, fear of
Howling

BARKING WHEN ALONE IN THE CAR

Problem: Whenever I leave my dog alone in the car, even for a few minutes, she barks and carries on something awful.

Why your dog is doing this: Your dog feels abandoned, and is barking in the hope you'll return and keep her company.

What to say and do:

1. Leave your dog in the car and walk away, then sneak back and hide nearby, ready to surprise your dog when she sounds off.

2. In the middle of a howl or bark, reappear suddenly. Verbally reprimand her and use the shaker can or spray bottle through a partially open window, or open the car door, do the scruff grip, and plunk her down on the seat.

3. After using one of the above methods, leave immediately and resume hiding. Repeat the correction as needed.

4. If your dog remains quiet for five minutes, return to the car, saying calmly as you approach, "What a good girl to be so quiet in the car." Open the door and stroke her slowly. Switch to a warning tone, saying, "You stay here and be quiet," and walk away. Increase the amount of time she can handle being alone in the car.

5. Don't leave a leash or a choke chain on your dog in the car. Your dog could get caught on something and strangle herself.

Why this works: Your dog is barking in the hope of bringing you back. If you return angry and upset, your dog will learn that barking only angers you.

Prevention: Do not leave your dog alone in the car for more than a few minutes, and make sure she is comfortable. Put a blanket down for security; it is essential that your dog has something soft to lie on, especially if she is in the back of a pickup or in a van. (It is illegal in some states for dogs to ride in the back of pickup trucks. If your dog must be in the back of your truck, make sure she is tethered in such a way that she cannot jump out over the edge and hang herself. Better yet, secure her crate in the truck bed and let her ride in it. Give her shelter from the sun and rain, and something soft to lie on.)

Practice her obedience lessons around the car and require her to do sit-stays before letting her get in or out of the car.

WARNINGS: Do not leave your dog in the car on a warm day. Your dog will die of heat exhaustion. Be sure your dog cannot activate automatic windows when she's alone in the car.

BATHING, MISBEHAVIOR DURING

Problem: My dog hates to be bathed. I can't even get her into the bathroom, let alone the tub.

Why your dog is doing this: Your dog may be scared because the tub floor is slippery or because the water is too hot or too cold. In previous bathing sessions, the soap may have irritated her eyes, or water may have dripped into her ears or nose. She might find getting in and out of the tub frightening. Also, some dogs just don't like water.

What to say and do:

1. Practice her obedience training in the house, and occasionally heel her into and out of the bathroom. As she becomes more comfortable in this situation, do some sit-stays in the bathroom and give her calming massages until she relaxes.

2. Spend time with her off-leash in the bathroom (not at her bath time). Feed her treats, give her calming massages, or just hang out there. When she relaxes, run some water into the tub while she is in there with you.

3. Get her used to going in and out of the tub when you have no intention of bathing her. Place a long rubber mat in the tub. If you have a large dog, climb into the tub first and encourage her to follow, tugging her leash gently to encourage her while you talk happily. Once she hops in, give her a treat or scatter some treats on the floor of the tub for her to find.

4. If she's too small to climb in, slowly and gently help her over the edge or lift her into the tub, making sure she feels secure throughout the process. Spend time in the tub with her (remember, the tub has no water in it yet), giving her a massage and feeding her treats. If she attempts to leap out, correct her and tell her to sit and stay. Then resume massage.

5. When she is relaxed about getting in the tub, a process that may take several days, get ready to bathe her. Put cotton in her ears and obtain a bland eye ointment from your veterinarian to protect her eyes from soap.

6. Put an extended shower head on the shower, so you can direct the spray at your dog. As you turn on the water, calmly reassure her that everything's okay and order her to stay. Keep one hand on her collar and, with the other, adjust the water, making certain she is not sprayed until the water temperature is just right (a lukewarm temperature is safe to use). It helps to have someone else—someone she knows well—hold her for you.

7. Very carefully wet her neck and back first, using very little pressure to allow her to get used to the water. The goal here is to keep her from becoming frightened. You don't even have to lather her the first time. Just wet, rub, and massage her, then end the session, particularly if she is not tolerating it well. If she's doing okay, proceed with a complete bath, again being very careful not to get soap in her eyes or water in her nose or ears. Use a washcloth to clean her head and face.

8. Dry her in the tub, then help her out and finish the job. Dogs usually love the post-tub toweling. Give her a treat and plenty of praise when you're finished. Allow her to run around the house—or outside if it's a warm day.

Why this works: This step-by-step approach allows your dog to overcome her fears gradually. The obedience lessons build her confidence and control.

Prevention: Avoid slippery tubs and floors, water that is too hot or too cold, and water or soap in her nose, mouth, eyes, or ears.

Your dog doesn't need to be bathed frequently, since bathing will strip her coat of its natural oils and cleansing capabilities. Regular brushing will maintain your dog better than bathing. If she is loaded with fleas or has rolled in some foul-smelling manure (that she thought was a lovely perfume!), a bath is in order. Use a good herbal flea soap rather than a chemical soap.

BEGGING AT MEALTIME

Problem: Whenever I sit down to eat, my dog begs for food.

Why is my dog doing this? Dogs are scavengers—that's probably why they were drawn to humans in the first place. They hung around campfires to eat our leftovers and they're still doing it today!

What to say and do:

1. Set up pretend meals for yourself when your dog is not hungry, so that you can both focus on the training session, and not on eating. The instant your dog begins to stare at you hungrily, tell him, "No begging!" in an authoritative voice. Shoo the dog away and say, "Go away!" Do this every time your dog hangs around food, whether you are eating or just unpacking groceries.

2. If that doesn't work, put him in a down-stay or teach him to go to his bed. (This must be taught in a separate lesson first, when there are no distractions.)

3. Take your dog by the collar or leash and lead him to his bed. Say, "Go to your bed and lie down," as you pat the bed and encourage him to settle in. Praise him for cooperating.

4. Tell him to stay on his bed and keep him there for three minutes. Then release him with calm praise. Repeat this procedure five or six times, and have him stay a bit longer each time until he understands "Go to your bed and lie down."

5. Build up the time he can remain on his bed, until you can actually eat a meal in peace.

Why this works: Teaching your dog to go to his bed allows him to understand what you want him to do. Whether you shoo him away, put him in a down-stay, or send him to his bed, consistency is the key here.

Prevention: Feed your dog his meal before you dine. If you want to offer him table scraps (as long as he's a hearty eater of his regular chow), put them in his bowl after his regular meal as a dessert. If you have small children who spill food or enjoy giving food to the dog, keep your dog out of the dining area during meals. Let him in after meals to clean up the floor. If you are feeding your dog once a day, increase it to two meals a day, so he won't get so hungry.

BEGGING FOR TREATS

Problem: Every time my dog sees anyone eating, he drools greedily. He also stares at the cupboard where his treats are kept.

Why your dog is doing this: Your dog, like most, is a little pig when it comes to food—especially people food.

What to say and do:

1. If your dog starts bothering you or anyone else for food, tell him, "No begging" in an annoyed voice, disgustedly shoo him away, and say, "Go away!"

2. If this doesn't work, put him in a down-stay. Be firm about making your dog control himself. If he continues to beg, send him to his bed or use the spray bottle or shaker can.

Why this works: Using the obedience commands to stop your dog from begging gives you a way to control him. If you're assertive, you will establish yourself as the lead dog, and this position gives you the right to keep him away from your food.

Prevention: Always feed your dog meals or treats in his bowl rather than from your hand. Don't feed him when he stares at the cupboard where his munchies are stored. Feed him a balanced, healthy diet. If he is on one meal a day, switch to two so he doesn't get so hungry. If he is being fed a proper diet, he is begging because he wants more food, not because he is starving or underfed.

BOARDING PROBLEMS

Problem: My dog hates to stay at the boarding kennel. The last time I took him there, I had to drag him trembling from the car to the building.

Why your dog is doing this: The kennel is a strange and scary place for your dog, and he fears being abandoned there, separated from you.

What to say and do:

1. Find a kennel that you like. The facilities as well as the people should meet your standards. It's important that the kennel managers let you see the entire operation. Explain your dog's special needs and ask if the managers can meet them.

2. Take your dog to visit the kennel several times. Let him meet everyone and hang around. Have the kennel staff feed him treats.

3. When he seems relaxed and eager to enter the kennel building and say hello to his new friends, leave him for a couple of hours only (expect to pay for this). Don't make your good-bye (or hello) a big deal. Tell him, "I'll be back in a couple of hours," and walk out. Leave him with some familiar bedding and a couple of chew toys.

4. Repeat this mini–boarding routine, adding time slowly until he becomes comfortable. Then leave him overnight. Board him regularly for a day or two even if you don't need to, until he's relaxed.

Why this works: Familiarizing your dog with the kennel will go a long way toward making him feel secure and comfortable when you actually leave him. Leaving him initially for short times lets him see that you will indeed return for him. His crate—his familiar bed—will offer him a sense of security.

Prevention: Make sure your dog is used to spending time alone in your home. Train him so that he feels comfortable and secure in his crate, which can also serve as his bed. Get him used to sleeping in the crate at night, for short periods during the day when you are home, and then while you're out. When you board him overnight, always take his crate along.

To prevent boredom while he's being boarded, find a kennel that can exercise him daily, either with long walks or with a romp in a fenced area. If he is well socialized, ask if he can play with other friendly dogs.

If he needs obedience training or needs to have his training reviewed, have the kennel staff work with him. Training sessions are a form of quality time that will help him fill his day. Make sure you trust the training methods they use, and ask for a demonstration.

Keep him on his usual diet to prevent stomach upsets. When you drop him off, provide the kennel with his food and any medications he needs. The fewer changes the better.

See also:
Afraid to be alone
Crate training

BOLTING FROM THE CAR

Problem: Whenever the car door is opened, my dog bolts out so fast I can't catch her. I'm afraid she's going to get hit.

Why your dog is doing this: Your dog thinks the end of the car ride means an exciting new place or an old familiar haunt, so she's in a big hurry to get out.

What to say and do:

1. Try to catch your dog in flight, grab her, quickly put her back in the car, and plunk her firmly down on the seat. Tell her, "No! Get back in the car. Shame on you! You stay!" If she tries to bolt again, correct her immediately with a scruff grip, and hold her firmly in place while you lecture her.

2. When she settles down, relax your grip and ease into a calming massage. Thank her for staying put.

3. If you are outside of the car when she tries to bolt, use the shaker can or the spray bottle to startle her and shoo her back in.

4. Always tell her to sit and stay and give her the hand signal before you open the door. Let her get out of the car only when you feel that it's safe to release her. Say, "Okay, you can get out of the car now—good girl."

5. If you are in the car, remind your dog to sit and stay before you open the door. If necessary, keep a leash on her for control, but make sure it doesn't get tangled and hurt her.

6. Routinely practice her obedience training around the car before you even get in. Require her to do several sit-stays next to the car while you open and shut the door. Let her get in only when she's calm. If she's very excited, take the time to massage her and help calm her. Remember to praise her for cooperating.

7. If she is very excitable, practice the training while the car is parked. When she's ready, go for very short drives around the block and review her training when you stop.

Why this works: Consistent firmness when she tries to escape will discourage her from bolting. Teaching her manners around your car in a structured way gives her a chance to learn to control herself even when she's excited.

Prevention: Obedience training will teach your dog to obey you. If you are consistent about safe car behavior, it will become a habit for your dog to wait for your okay before getting into or out of the car. Never let your dog jump in or out without a specific invitation from you. Always remind your dog to stay before you open the door.

See also:
Jumping out of the car window

BOLTING OUT OF THE HOUSE

Problem: My dog sometimes dashes out the door. I'm afraid he's going to get hit by a car.

Why your dog is doing this: If your dog is bored or isn't getting enough exercise, he'll dash outside just to stretch his legs and check out the neighborhood. This is especially true for dogs who don't have large fenced yards or who are confined to a leash all the time.

What to say and do:

1. Sneak up on your dog. Slip outside without your dog seeing you and hide about 10 feet from the door. Be armed with a couple of shaker cans, and have a helper inside the house to open your front door.

2. When your dog makes his escape, jump out at him, yell angrily, "Get back in the house! Go home!" and shake or throw the cans at him. Startle him as you chase him back into the house. This may sound cruel, but your dog must accept that you get angry with him when he bolts. A far worse fate awaits him if he gets hit by a car.

3. Retreat to your hiding place, leaving the front door open. If your dog comes out again, repeat the correction. Show him that you are sincerely upset. The consequences of not taking you seriously could cost him his life.

4. If he remains in the house for five minutes, go inside and speak calmly and praisingly: "Good boy to stay in the house. Thank you!" Then switch to a warning tone: "You stay home. Stay in the house," and go out again, leaving the door open. If he even thinks about leaving, shake the can and yell at him. Repeat this exercise at random times.

5. Practice the sit-stay at the front door. Make him stay while you rattle the doorknob and open and shut the door. When you take him outside, always go through doorways first, making him stay until you say, "Okay!" If necessary, when he's in the house, leave a leash on him that you can step on if he tries to bolt out the door.

6. Before you open the door for guests, caution him to stay in the house and give the shaker can a little rattle. If necessary, put him on a leash when guests arrive.

Why this works: If your dog gets an unpleasant surprise as he bolts out the door, he's going to think twice before he does it again. Practicing the obedience training will establish you as pack leader and will teach him to take you seriously. If he gets enough exercise and socialization, he won't be so desperate to dash out into the world.

Prevention: Incorporate your dog into your life more. Play with him and take him for walks, car rides, and romps in the park. Include him on outings with friends. Make sure he gets plenty of exercise daily; if possible find him a doggy playmate to romp with. Practice his obedience work all over the house and yard. Repeatedly bring him into the house from outside, using the come command. Require that he sit and stay while you open the door and step through first. Spend quiet times with him doing massage and calming work, and let him sleep in the house at night, in your room if possible.

See also:
Off-leash misbehavior
Roaming
Running away

BRUSHING, MISBEHAVIOR DURING

Problem: When I try to brush my dog, he snaps at the brush and fidgets, refusing to stand still.

Why your dog is doing this: He dislikes the sensation of the brush and lets you know this by squirming and nipping.

What to say and do:

1. Never use a wire slicker brush; unless used expertly, this brush can pull and tweak a dog's hair and skin. Instead, use soft-bristle brushes, like the ones used on cats or babies.

2. Keep a leash and collar on your dog, and have him sit facing away from you. If he is small, put him on your lap or on a table. Calm him by gently massaging his neck, shoulders, and back. When he's relaxed, stroke him gently with the brush and your hand at the same time. If he struggles, make him hold still and settle him with massage before resuming.

3. Press firmly enough with the brush so as not to tickle him. The brush is soft, so you won't hurt him.

4. Keep your first sessions short, stopping before he tires of it—five minutes, maximum. Give him a treat and repeat the procedure later.

5. Once your dog realizes that brushing doesn't hurt, slowly work your way around his body, leaving the sensitive areas (back of the legs, inside the thighs, behind his ears, in his armpits) for later when he is fully accustomed to being brushed.

6. If he is matted, proceed slowly and deliberately. If you hurry, you are likely to pull his hair and lose the trust you are developing. Be gentle and respectful of his body and speak to him softly while you work.

7. If he is restless, give him something to chew while you brush. Initially a friend or family member may need to hold the dog and the toy while you work.

Why this works: Controlling and calming your dog before you begin to brush establishes a positive and comforting mood. Using a soft brush and proceeding slowly allows your dog to become accustomed to your careful, respectful handling.

Prevention: Use a soft brush, and move your hands slowly and deliberately. Early handling lessons for puppies will teach them to accept restraint and will prepare them for being groomed. Visit a pet store and check out the grooming tools. If you have a heavily coated dog, you can use de-matting tools and lotions after your dog learns to enjoy the soft brush. Relax before you begin brushing. Your dog will sense that you are calm, and he will calm down, too.

CAR, FEAR OF

Problem: My dog is afraid to get in the car. I have to drag him or lift him in.

Why your dog is doing this: Cars can be hard for some dogs to get into. If your dog banged himself getting in, if the door slammed and scared him, or if he was helped in clumsily, he will naturally be afraid to get in again. If his experiences with the car have been unpleasant—if he gets carsick, if he's been left in the car alone for long periods, or if he's put in the car only to go to the veterinarian—he will not want to get in again.

What to say and do:

1. Put your dog on a leash and have some treats ready. Give him one of the treats and lead him toward the car. Say happily, "Let's get in the car. Come on, good boy."

2. If he hangs back, don't drag him. Instead, pat your leg and lure him to you with the treats and happy talk. Give gentle little tugs to the leash and pat your legs as you invite him for a calming massage and a treat.

3. Once you reach the car, open the door, still chatting happily. Lean in and pat the seat, saying excitedly, "Come on, get in the car." Hold the treat just inside the car, so he will reach for it. At this point, your dog may climb in on his own. If he does, praise him lavishly. If he does not, try climbing in first; he will probably follow.

4. If he doesn't make any attempt to get in, gently place one of his front legs on either the floor or the seat, depending on his size. Make him hold that position while you scratch his back, offer him another treat, and chatter happily, "Good boy. It's good to get in the car." When he relaxes, put the other front leg in and repeat the rub, reassurances, and treat.

5. When he relaxes, lift his hindquarters in gently, firmly holding his thighs to support his body weight evenly. Praise him warmly for being so brave and cooperative. Once he's in the car, give him another treat, scratch him in his favorite places, and happily ask him to come out. Praise him for doing so well.

6. Immediately repeat the entire in-and-out procedure as many times as necessary until he gets in pretty much by himself. It usually only takes a few times for him to feel comfortable. A good tip: scatter some treats around the car and encourage him to hunt for them.

7. Spend some time with him in the car while it is parked. Give him a calming massage and hang out until he's relaxed. Let him experience being in the car as something pleasant and as something he can do with you.

8. If he is still frightened of the car, try feeding him his meals in it, or leave the car door open and let him explore the car on his own (make sure you do this in a safe place away from other cars).

Why this works: Teaching your dog to get in the car with gentle guidance, massage, and treats gives him a new—and more enjoyable—perspective on the car. Making him comfortable during the ride will help make the car less scary for him.

Prevention: Make sure your dog has a comfortable place to ride, so he will enjoy being in the car. Take care that the sun isn't beating down on him through a window. Provide him with a cozy bed, especially if he is riding in a cargo van or a truck. If he must ride in the back of an open pickup—a very dangerous practice—make sure he is securely tethered so he cannot jump over the edge and hang himself, an all-too-common and wholly unnecessary occurrence. Also make sure he has adequate shelter from the rain and sun. It is illegal in some states to drive with a dog loose in the back of a pickup.

CARSICKNESS

Problem: When my dog rides in the car, he get sick and vomits.

Why your dog is doing this: Your dog may have a weak stomach just like some humans. If he has seldom been in a car, or if his past experiences have been traumatic (a trip to the veterinarian, groomer, or boarding kennel), he may become physically ill from stress.

What to say and do:

1. Spend time with your dog in the car while it is parked. Put some of his bedding on the seat, and give him a toy. Give him a calming massage, and don't rush. You may need a week of daily sessions for this training to work.

2. When he's relaxed during one of your car visits, run the engine for a few minutes. (Don't do this in an enclosed garage!) Do this until he is oblivious to it, and always end the session with a calming massage.

3. Once your dog is comfortable spending time in the car when it is parked, take him for a short drive, but make sure his stomach is empty. Open the windows so there is plenty of fresh air, but don't roll them down all the way. You don't want him to jump out.

4. Drive to a nearby park or patch of grass and play with your dog. If there are no parks nearby, simply drive around the block, and have a play session when you get back home. Repeat this process, gradually increasing the length of the trip as your dog relaxes.

Why this works: Allowing your dog to get used to a parked car helps settle his tummy. Very short rides with fun endings will keep him from associating car rides with unpleasant situations. Every time he arrives somewhere without having gotten nauseated, it helps break the pattern of carsickness.

Prevention: Make sure he never has a full stomach when you take him on rides, and see that he relieves himself beforehand.

Always keep a window open so he'll have plenty of fresh air.

If your dog is crate-trained, try transporting him in his crate. The sense of security he feels in his crate may lower his anxiety level and prevent him from getting sick.

Make sure the sun isn't beating down on him through a window.

Making a bed for your dog on the floor of the car might help, as there is less rolling motion on the floor.

If all else fails, ask your vet's advice.

CHASING BICYCLES

Problem: My dog loves to run after bicycles, barking and trying to nip the tires or ankles of the rider.

Why your dog is doing this: Remember, dogs are pack animals, and chasing is instinctive. Your dog might want to bring down the bicycle just as she would bring down a deer in the wild, or chase it away should she decide it is intruding in her territory.

What to say and do:

1. If your dog has never had a chance to check out a bicycle close up, let her do so. Once she realizes the bicycle is inanimate and not that exciting, she may lose her desire to chase it.

2. Have a friend hold the bicycle still while you practice some basic obedience commands. When your dog has her attention focused on you, have your friend walk the bicycle around in circles 15 feet away (not around you) while you keep your dog's attention on the training.

3. If your dog focuses on the bike (watch her ears—they'll perk up), give her a sharp yank on her leash, ordering her in a low, menacing voice, "Leave it!" Praise her as soon as she directs her attention back to you and have her sit. Tell her, "Good girl, sit. Good sit. Good to leave the bike alone." Then calm her with a massage.

4. Resume the drill; be very liberal with praise. Every time she looks at the bike, correct her. If she ignores your voice and leash correction, get her attention with the shaker can or spray bottle. Then have her sit and calm her with some massage.

5. After she learns to ignore the bicycle while your friend is walking it, have your friend ride it in circles (at a distance). Carry on the obedience work, corrections, and massage until she ignores the bicycle. Remember to praise her for controlling herself.

6. Next, ask your friend to ride the bicycle out of sight for a minute or two and return to ride past you. If your dog fixates on the bicycle, use the shaker can or spray bottle before she gets in motion and growl, "Leave it!" Praise her for looking away from the bicycle.

7. Repeat until your dog ignores the bicycle. Then take her to a park frequented by bicyclists. As soon as your dog notices a bicyclist approaching, caution her firmly: "Leave it." Make her sit and calm her after the bike passes. If she is having trouble being good, put her through a quick obedience drill to get her attention back to you.

8. If she totally ignores the approaching bicyclist, praise her warmly: "Good girl to leave bicycles alone."

9. If you can recruit friends to ride past your dog, provide them with a spray bottle and instructions on how to use it, and have them spritz her if she tries to chase them.

Why this works: By first making your dog control herself around a bicycle that is not as tempting to chase, you will be making it easier for her to ignore bicycles that whiz past her. This gives you a chance to correct her while she is thinking about chasing, before her body is in motion. Startling her with the shaker can the instant she thinks about bicycles will go a long way toward discouraging her from chasing them. You are telling her very clearly that it is bad to chase, good to stop, good to sit, and good to be calm, which you help her do with the massage.

Prevention: Do not allow your dog to run loose around bicycles. Keep her leashed. Start obedience training early and practice the commands routinely, so your dog will take you seriously when you address her.

Early socialization—walks around the block or to the park—will gradually desensitize her to passing bicyclists. This technique works for skateboarders, rollerskaters, and youngsters on tricycles as well.

Play with your dog in the park. Give her fun things to do other than chasing bicycles. Teach her to chase Frisbees or tennis balls to satisfy her chasing instincts.

Make sure she gets enough exercise. A tired dog will be less inclined to chase things.

CHASING CARS

Problem My dog loves to chase cars. I know he's going to cause an accident one day or get himself killed.

Why your dog is doing this: Dogs are pack animals, and it is instinctive for them to chase things that move. In the wild they had to run down their dinner. Your dog is chasing cars because they move, because they are invading his territory, and because it's fun.

What to say and do:

1. Car chasing is a difficult habit to break. The simplest solution is not to let your dog run loose. A firm foundation in obedience training is necessary. Otherwise your dog will not take you seriously when you correct him. Practice the obedience commands in and around your house until your dog listens to you. Work with him until he is capable of doing thirty-minute down-stays on-leash indoors.

2. Next, take him outside and casually stand on the sidewalk, keeping the leash loose. Have the shaker can or spray bottle with you. The instant your dog alerts to a car (his ears will perk up), snap the leash several times in rapid succession, shake the can noisily in his face or spray him, and tell him in an urgent tone, "No! Leave it!" Yank, shake or spray, glare and yell for five to ten seconds.

3. When your dog looks humbled, order him to sit, and praise him for responding correctly. Then calm him with a brief massage. Repeat this procedure many times over several days or weeks. At some point your dog will see an oncoming car and quickly look away. At that moment, praise your dog warmly for ignoring the car.

4. Once your dog is able to ignore cars while on a 6-foot leash, graduate to a 15-foot leash. Stand around casually and don't pay any attention to him. The instant he fixates on a car, snap the leash and throw the shaker can at him. As he learns to control himself, practice on longer leashes, but make sure he can't run out in front of a car.

5. If this technique does not work, set up a surprise attack from your car. As the dog approaches the car, jump out and douse him with water from a bucket, a water balloon, or a large squirt gun, or fire a barrage of shaker cans at him. Be scary and abrupt, or your dog won't learn that cars are scary and can "attack" him back.

6. If even this technique has no effect, get the help of a professional trainer with a remote-controlled electric-shock collar. As drastic as this sounds, it is harmless in the long run, and it could prevent your dog from being killed or causing an accident.

Why this works: By correcting your dog for just *looking* at cars, you are letting him know you don't want him to even *think* about chasing them. By combining the correction with obedience training and massage, you are letting him know it's bad to chase, good to sit, and good to calm down.

Prevention: Do not let your dog run loose. Exercise him off-leash in a safe area away from the street, which is no place for him to be roaming in the first place. Give him enough exercise, training, companion time, playtime, and attention.

The best prevention for car chasing is a nice, big, secure yard, with a solid fence. However, if this is not possible for you, make sure to routinely take him to the park or on jogs with you, so he gets enough exercise. Routinely practice his obedience training on the sidewalk, and insist that he pay attention to you. Play with him there, so he can have fun without chasing cars. Teach him to fetch, so he can chase something acceptable.

CHASING CATS, OTHER PEOPLE'S

Problem: Whenever my dog sees a cat, he lunges at it. If he's off-leash, he chases it.

Why your dog is doing this: Chasing small animals is instinctive for dogs. As hunters, dogs revel in the thrill of the chase.

What to say and do:

1. Chasing cats can be difficult to stop. It is essential for your dog to master a few obedience commands. Practice the commands for a week or so before addressing the cat-chasing problem.

2. Take your dog out for a walk. Keep him on your left side, and hold the leash in your left hand. In your right hand carry the shaker can or spray bottle.

3. The instant your dog sees a cat (his ears will perk up excitedly) say, "Leave it!" in a deep voice and snap the leash sharply as you shake the can or spray water in your dog's face). If possible, do this just as your dog is about to bark or lunge at the cat.

4. If your dog calms down and looks humbled, praise him soothingly and say, "Good boy. Good to leave the kitty alone." Make your dog sit and stay and give him a calming massage. Alternate between the correction and the praise and calming massage, as needed. The faster you correct him when he thinks "cat!" the better.

5. Be ready to correct your dog even if the cat is a block away. It is very useful to remain at a distance from the cat, controlling and calming your dog for as long as it takes for him relax and lose interest in the cat.

6. Heel your dog closer to the cat. Practice lots of sits and stays, as you go. Keep his attention on you and praise him liberally. Remember to correct him as soon as he perks up his ears.

Why this works: Anticipating when your dog is thinking about chasing the cat, and correcting him immediately, is much more effective than correcting him after he's begun running. Obedience work teaches your dog to take your commands seriously, and calming him gives him a mellow mood to return to.

Prevention: Never encourage your dog to "get the kitty" or any other small creature. Try to socialize your dog with some friendly cats when he's still a pup. This way, he will think of small animals as friendly playmates, not as prey.

Make sure he gets plenty of exercise, and if he likes to chase things, teach him to retrieve a ball or a Frisbee.

Try to stop your dog the instant he perks up his ears, while he is still thinking of chasing the cat, and before his body is actually in motion. Before you can have any success off-leash, you must teach your dog to respect cats when he's on-leash.

CHASING CATS, YOUR OWN

Problem: My dog loves to chase my cat; my poor kitty has been hiding out behind and on top of everything.

Why your dog is doing this: It's your dog's natural instinct to chase other animals. As hunters, dogs love the thrill of the chase.

What to say and do:

1. Review the obedience commands and do a daily calming massage for at least a week before attempting to correct the cat-chasing problem.

2. Grab a spray bottle, put a leash and collar on your dog, and take him into a large room. Put your cat at the other end of the room on a couch where she'll feel safe. Have a helper calmly stroke the cat. If you don't have a helper, put your cat on something high, like a cabinet or a chest of drawers.

3. The instant your dog spots the cat and perks his ears up, correct him by snapping the leash sharply and spraying him with water. Tell him firmly, "You leave kitty alone!" Make your dog sit and calm him with massage. Praise him for sitting quietly and ignoring the cat. Say "Good to leave the kitty alone."

4. Repeat this procedure until he gives up and ignores your cat. Be consistent and quick with your correction. Go immediately into the massage if he responds to the correction.

5. Heel your dog closer to your cat, continuing the correction and calming routine, until you end up with two fairly relaxed animals at opposite ends of the couch.

6. When your dog can ignore your cat while she is sitting still, it is time to teach him to ignore her when the cat is moving. Have your helper nudge your cat away, and repeat the correction and calming sequence with the dog until your cat can meander about the room while your dog ignores her.

7. Once your dog has learned this lesson on-leash, try it off-leash.

8. Practice this technique in different rooms so your dog learns that these rules apply everywhere.

Why this works: By teaching your dog to respect your cat first at a distance and then moving closer, you are helping him learn self-control. The calming massage in between corrections helps your dog relax and mellow out.

Prevention: Never let your dog think his cat-chasing is amusing.

Give your cat a safe place to eat and keep her litter box away from your dog.

Spend as much quiet time as possible with the dog and cat in the same room.

Keep your dog on a leash in the house, when you are there to supervise, until he learns to ignore the cat.

CHASING JOGGERS

Problem: My dog thinks joggers exist just so she can chase them. She runs up to them as if she's going to attack them.

Why your dog is doing this: Chasing is fun! Your dog could also be chasing intruders away from what she has claimed as her territory—which she may decide is wherever she happens to be!

What to say and do:

1. Establish a strong foundation in obedience training before you try to correct this problem. Practice the obedience commands daily, especially the sit-stay and down-stay. Get your dog to the point where you can put her on a stay command (on-leash) while you walk, and then jog in a 15-foot circle around her.

2. When she's ready, get a helper to jog slowly in a circle about 15 feet from where you are doing the obedience training. Praise your dog continually as you work with her. If she alerts to the jogger and her ears perk up, correct her with a sharp leash snap and forcefully tell her to "Leave it!" Praise her for returning her attention to you, saying, "Good girl to leave it." Have her sit, and calm her with massage. If she ignores your correction, add the shaker can or spray bottle.

3. Have the jogger run past you several times while your dog is being calmed in a sit-stay by your side. Correct her sharply and shake the can at her if she shows any interest in the jogger.

4. Put your dog in a sit-stay at the end of the 6-foot leash and have the jogger trot by. Correct any break from the sit-stay by plunking your dog firmly back in the same spot. When she can handle that, put her on a 15-foot line and repeat the exercise.

5. When she seems ready, go to a jogging trail and stand with your dog off to the side, 50 to 100 feet away and put her through an obedience session with calming work on the sits. Be fun and upbeat. Remember, you have to be more fun than the joggers. If she looks at them and her ears perk up, correct her sharply and use the spray bottle or shaker can if necessary. Praise her, make her sit, and calm her.

6. Now move closer to the jogging trail by half the distance and hang out casually, keeping the leash loose. If your dog's ears perk up, correct her. If she looks but her ears don't perk up, tell her "Good to leave it!" and praise her. Stay there until she's bored with the joggers. Repeat the sessions at frequent intervals until she's cured of the habit.

7. Remember, fun is the key here! Take a favorite chew toy to the jogging trail so that your dog will have more fun playing with you than she would chasing the joggers.

Why this works: Obedience training and teaching your dog to control herself around joggers gives you a chance to stay one step ahead of her and correct her for even thinking about chasing. The calming work helps her relax. You are telling her very clearly that it's bad to chase, good to stop, good to sit, and good to calm down.

Prevention: Don't let your dog run loose. If you can't be outside with your dog, keep her in a spacious, securely fenced yard with toys to play with and gnaw on, a sandbox for digging, and a wading pool to splash in.

Watch your dog's ears. When they perk up, she is thinking "Jogger!" This is the best time to correct her.

Make sure she gets plenty of exercise so she won't chase joggers just to let off steam. If she likes to chase things, teach her to retrieve a Frisbee, a stick, or a ball.

CHASING LIVESTOCK

Problem: My dog chases livestock. I'm afraid he's going to get hurt by an animal or, worse, shot by a farmer.

Why your dog is doing this: It is a natural instinct for dogs to chase other animals. In the wild, bringing down game provided dogs with food, and our domesticated dogs still thrill to the excitement of the hunt.

What to say and do:

1. Practice your obedience work around your house and yard until your dog automatically obeys your commands. Then practice outside of a corral where some animals, preferably the type he likes to chase, are quietly standing around. Practice long down-stays adjacent to the corrals or pens, building him up to a thirty-minute down-stay.

2. The moment your dog fixates on the animals and perks up his ears, give him several leash snaps, rattle the shaker can at him, and say in a serious tone, "Leave it! You leave those animals alone!" Make him sit, and praise him when he does.

3. If he can't take his mind off the animals, put him through a firm and rapid obedience session with lots of quick sits. Every time he looks at the animals, correct him with leash snaps, shaker can, and your voice.

4. When he gives you his attention, give him a nice long massage while you sit near the corral, left hand massaging, right hand holding the leash, ready to correct him the instant his ears perk up. You can also correct him by switching to a scruff grip with your massage hand.

5. Practice around the barnyard and corrals until your dog is no longer interested in the animals, but keep him away from all livestock in between training sessions.

6. When your dog has learned to ignore the livestock while they stand around quietly, have a helper go into the pens or corrals and chase the animals around a bit. If the chickens flutter or squawk, or if the goats, cows, or horses trot around a bit, your dog's interest will be sparked again. At the slightest show of interest, correct him very firmly. When he ignores the animals while they are running around, praise him.

7. Keep him on-leash until he understands that he must ignore the animals. Then let him drag the leash in the barnyard area while the animals are penned and quiet. Be ready to correct him if he tries to bolt after them, or if he shows any interest whatsoever.

8. If this doesn't work, find a professional trainer who uses a remote-controlled collar that will administer a slight shock to your dog while he's in the act of chasing. This may seem cruel, but the discomfort is minimal compared to your dog getting kicked or gored by livestock or shot by a farmer. It could also prevent him from killing or mauling someone's animals.

Why this works: Obedience training teaches your dog to respect you and take you seriously. Starting out in a controlled situation allows you to stay one step ahead of him. By anticipating his reactions, you can correct him for even thinking about chasing. The correction lets him know you disapprove of his actions, and the massage calms him.

Prevention: Don't let your dog run loose. Even if you live on a 30-acre estate, it only takes your dog fifteen seconds to bound away and harass your neighbor's livestock. When you can't be outside with your dog, keep him in a spacious fenced yard. Even if you live in the country, a fenced yard is an absolute necessity. If your dog has killed or maimed livestock, you may never be able to break him of this habit.

CHEWING FURNITURE AND WALLS

Problem: My dog loves to gnaw on chair legs, rip out the couch stuffing, and chew the walls and woodwork.

Why your dog is doing this: Your dog may be chewing for a number of reasons. If he's a puppy, he may be teething. If he's grown, he may be bored and lonely, or he may view these objects as toys. When he rips the stuffing out of the couch, he is duplicating the stripping of dinner off a carcass in the wild.

What to do and say:

1. If you catch your dog chewing on the walls or furniture, startle him with a firm "No!" and smack the object he was chewing on. Remember, hit the object; never hit the dog. As you slap the object, lecture him firmly. If necessary, do the scruff grip, too. Then soften your voice and guide the dog to an acceptable toy, praising him.

2. Get a product called Bitter Apple or Thums and dab some on the walls and furniture. Both products taste very bad to dogs and will deter chewing. For many offenders, that's all you'll need to do to solve the chewing problem.

3. If you find something destroyed after the fact—if you come home and find the living room covered in cushion stuffing, for example—you can't effectively correct your dog. You can, though, try to act as unconcerned as possible (which can be a great challenge), wait for your dog to return to the great fun of demolishing the place, and then ambush and correct him.

Why this works: Monitoring your dog closely allows you to correct him the instant he puts his mouth on something unacceptable—the only fair and effective time to correct and teach him. By guiding him to an acceptable toy every time he needs to chew, you are letting him know what is, and is not, okay to chew on.

Prevention: Don't leave your dog unattended in any area where he can get into trouble, even for brief moments, until he's cured of this habit. Put him in a pen, a section of the basement, a crate, or the yard when you can't watch him.

Make sure he has several things to chew on. Dogs like to chew on wood, so providing natural sticks will give him something other than the chair legs to chew on. Don't give him processed wood, because it will splinter. Cow hoofs or a large, sturdy beef marrow or knuckle bone will keep him occupied for hours.

Give your dog plenty of daily exercise. If he is tired from a long run in the park or a romp with a doggy friend, he's less likely to gnaw on everything.

See also:
Crate training

CHEWING IN THE CAR

Problem: My dog ate through the armrest of my car—this problem is out of control!

Why your dog is doing that: Your dog thinks the car upholstery is one big chew toy. It's supple, it's tasty, and it's long-lasting.

What to say and do:

1. Leave your dog in the car with a chew toy and walk away. Sneak back, hide out, and watch him. When he starts to gnaw on the car upholstery, open the car door quickly, give him a firm scruff grip, and lecture him: "Shame on you! Bad dog!" At the same time, smack the part of the car (never the dog) that he was chewing. Give him a chew toy, caution him to be good, and return to your hiding place.

2. If he needs to be corrected again, do so. If he remains good for five minutes, return calmly to the car and talk to him sweetly.

3. If this technique doesn't work, use the shaker can to startle him when you correct him.

4. If your dog continues to be destructive, crate-train him indoors. When he calmly accepts the crate, keep him crated in the car when you aren't able to monitor him.

Why this works: Only by catching your dog in the act of chewing can you correct this behavior. It does no good to scold your dog after the fact. He will only get confused and think that his greeting to you upon your return is what is making you angry.

Replacing the forbidden object with an acceptable chew toy helps him understand what is okay, and what is not okay, to chew on.

Prevention: If your dog is chewing destructively in your house, correct that problem first. Make sure your dog has his own chew toys and guide him to them frequently. Smear foul-tasting products such as Bitter Apple on the arm rest and other protruding parts of your car's interior.

Don't leave your dog alone in the car for long periods, especially when he's young. Boredom and lack of exercise will lead to excessive chewing.

Practice obedience work in and around your car.

And remember, *never leave your dog in the car on a warm day.* Even with the windows opened, a car can heat up to a lethal temperature in just a few minutes and kill your dog..

CHEWING PLANTS

Problem: My dog is ruining my garden and houseplants. He strips the bushes, lies in my flower bed, snacks on my vegetables, eats the houseplants, and digs in the pots.

Why your dog is doing this: Wolves and coyotes graze on medicinal plants to stay healthy. This instinct endures in our dogs, so they munch on plants. It's natural for your dog to chew on branches and leaves—that's what he would do in the wild.

What to say and do:

1. Fence off your most sacred garden plants, and put your houseplants out of reach. Wrap chicken wire around some garden plants, and lay it around the roots if your dog is digging.

2. Give your dog a piece of natural wood—a stick or small branch, for example—to chew on, but no processed wood, as that can splinter.

3. If you catch your dog chewing on a plant, startle him with a reprimand—"Leave it!"—and use the shaker can, spray bottle, or scruff grip, if necessary. Then give him something he's allowed to chew on and play with him and his new toy.

4. If your dog is lying contentedly in your flower bed, contemplating destruction, tell him, "Come on, get out of there!" Shoo him away, show him where he can lie down, praise him as he leaves, and give him a toy.

Why this works: By limiting your dog's access to plants, you make certain he can't destroy them. And by correcting him when you catch him, you give him a clear message that this behavior is unacceptable.

Prevention: Fence off sacred plants, but do not put the dog in a tiny pen. He needs room to run around; flowers don't. Give him plenty of acceptable chew toys, a sandbox, and a wading pool to keep him busy and happy in the yard. Put your houseplants out of his reach when you can't watch him.

See also:
Digging

CHEWING YOUR BELONGINGS WHEN YOU'RE HOME

Problem: My dog destroys my things! Last night she chewed a hole in the couch, and last week she ate a pair of my shoes.

Why your dog is doing this: Chewing releases excess energy, and if your dog doesn't know what is and is not acceptable to chew on, she will destroy your house. The younger the dog, the more intense the need to chew. Chewing is necessary during the teething period, from approximately three months old to ten months old.

What to say and do:

1. If you catch your dog chewing your things, correct her firmly. Tell her, "No! This is not your toy!" and take the object from her *gently.* Hit the forbidden object (not the dog) a few times, repeating your firm words. Then switch your voice to a sweet tone. Guide her to an acceptable toy and say, "This is your toy. You can play with this." *Warning:* Never approach your dog harshly and corner her or scare her. She might become frightened and defend herself aggressively. Remember, you are her teacher. Always be kind.

2. Leave the forbidden object on the floor and watch your dog closely. If she goes back to it, correct her verbally again. If your words have no effect, use the scruff grip or shaker can. Guide her to what she can have. When you can't watch her, place the forbidden object out of her reach.

3. If you find something destroyed after the fact, leave it on the floor and say nothing to her until she returns to it, as most dogs will. Correct her the instant she puts her mouth on it, and then guide her to her own toys.

4. Don't leave her unattended in the house, even for fifteen minutes. Confine her in a crate, pen, or yard, and give her something acceptable to chew on.

5. Apply foul-tasting solutions to things that you can't remove like walls, cabinets, piano legs, and couches. Bitter Apple, Thums, or Tabasco sauce will discourage chewing. Sprinkle pepper on linoleum or carpet edges.

6. Immediately mend any holes in pillows or couches to reduce the temptation for your dog to return to it.

7. Children's toys are very tempting to puppies. Don't let pups into rooms full of toys, as your pup can't tell the difference between these toys and her own. Give kids a separate play area.

Why this works: Monitoring your dog very closely enables you to correct her the instant she goes to chew the wrong things. Confining her when you can't watch her closely prevents her from selecting your things to chew on.

Prevention: Dogproof your dog's special area, your house, and your yard. Remove anything that might hurt your dog—electrical cords, cleansers, antifreeze, slug bait, poisonous plants, and so on.

Provide your dog with an assortment of acceptable toys wherever she goes in your house and yard, and encourage her to play with them. Provide a toy box so your dog will know where to find them.

Obedience training will calm your dog and teach her to respect you and take you seriously, so that she will listen to you when you correct her for chewing. Practice indoors, especially where your dog has destroyed things. Long down-stays next to gnawed walls and couches are helpful.

Make sure your dog gets plenty of exercise. A tired dog will have less energy for chewing. Bored dogs are likely to chew, so make sure your dog has an interesting daily routine.

See also:
Crate training

CHEWING YOUR BELONGINGS WHEN YOU'RE OUT

Problem: When I leave my dog alone in the house, she always destroys something. Last time it was my address book and a candle.

Why your dog is doing this: Your dog may be chewing because she's bored, or she may have been given too much freedom before she knew what was acceptable to chew on, so she views your house as a playground. Also, during the teething period (approximately three to ten months), chewing is a natural and important activity.

What to say and do:

1. You must teach your dog to respect your things when you are home, before you can even begin to trust her when you are out. As the pack leader, you must make clear to her what she may and may not chew on.

2. If you come home and find something chewed, ignore the crime and greet your dog normally, no matter how angry you are. Don't correct your dog as you walk in the door, because at that instant she is not being destructive, and she'll misinterpret what she's being corrected for. Wait until she returns to the scene of the crime and begins to sniff or grab at the destroyed item again. At that instant say, "No! Shame on you," and smack the object (never the dog). For added emphasis, with headstrong dogs, you can use the scruff grip or the shaker can.

3. Give her an acceptable chew toy and say, "Here, chew on this." Watch her, and if she returns to the forbidden object, reprimand her again.

4. You can crate your dog if you go out for two or three hours. For longer periods, you may need to dogproof a room, set up an exercise pen, or provide a place for her in the basement. If your yard is fenced and secure, let her stay outside in pleasant weather, providing, of course, a suitable shelter and toys.

5. Apply a commercial chew repellent to immovable things your dog likes to chew. Thums and Bitter Apple both work.

Why this works: The only effective way to correct your dog is to catch her in the act of chewing. Waiting for her to return to her destructive activities gives you an opportunity to correct her instantly.

Prevention: Don't leave your dog in a place where there are unacceptable things to chew on.

Make sure your dog gets plenty of exercise, so she's tired when you leave her. Give her toys and play with her with them.

Prepare a dogproof area that is free from hazards such as electrical cords, cleaning products, and antifreeze, and confine your dog when you are not around. And provide her with chew toys—always.

See also:
Crate training

CHILDREN, BEING WILD WITH. SEE PLAYING TOO EXUBERANTLY WITH KIDS

CRATE TRAINING

Problem: I put my dog in his new crate, and in just a few seconds he was frantic to get out.

Why your dog is doing this: Confining your dog in a crate without giving him a chance to get used to it makes him feel trapped. He has been separated from his pack family, so he tries to claw his way out or call for help. Also, if he has ever been confined to a crate at the vet's office or on a plane, his memory of that experience will contribute to his anxiety.

What to say and do:

1. You want the crate to become a secure den for your dog, so you must introduce him to it gradually. Put the crate in a room where you spend a lot of time. Prop the door open so he won't bump into it, and line the floor of the crate with cozy bedding.

2. Let your dog check out the crate on his own. Toss in his toys or some treats and encourage him to go inside. Praise him lavishly as he steps through the door. Repeat this procedure several times a day until he feels at home in his crate.

3. When he is nosing around the crate or resting inside it, scratch him in his favorite places or give him a calming massage.

When he seems relaxed, quickly close and open the door in between scratches to get him used to the sound it makes.

4. When he seems very relaxed with the crate, it is time to close the door. Make sure he has relieved himself before you do this. Nudge him in gently, and be sure he has a toy to chew on. Reach in and give him a calming massage, and then close the crate door.

5. Sit in front of the crate, and if he starts to scratch or whine, correct him instantly. Bang on the front of the crate and tell him "Quiet!" You can also use the shaker can or spray bottle to correct him. If he remains quiet for one minute, let him out, calmly praising him. Put him back in immediately with encouraging words, and leave him there for three minutes.

6. Slowly increase the amount of time he is crated, until you can leave him in for fifteen minutes. Stay in sight until he's relaxed, and then wander in and out of the room. When he's comfortable with that, you can begin to get him used to being crated when you are not home. Start with short outings—fifteen minutes maximum—and build up slowly.

7. If your dog is too anxious to handle this method, you must obedience-train him first, or review his training, especially the long down-stays. Build him up until he is able to do fifteen-minute down-stays outside the crate. Follow steps 1 through 3, above, so that he is comfortable with the crate.

8. With his leash on, do several two- to three-minute down-stays next to the crate. Then encourage him to go into his crate, and while he's there, have him do a one-minute down-stay. If he is nervous, make him stay down, but do some calming massage on him. Release him cheerfully, let him come out, and praise him. Repeat this procedure several times in a row, increasing the amount of time gradually until he is comfortable doing a five-minute down-stay.

9. When he is comfortable with the five-minute down-stay, it is time to practice with the door closed and the leash passed through it. Start with a one-minute down-stay, and very gradually build up to fifteen minutes. If he acts up, correct him with a leash snap as you tell him, "No! Down and stay." Praise him warmly when you release him.

10. When he seems comfortable, take the leash off and repeat step 9. Give him something to chew on while he's crated and build up the amount of time slowly while you remain in the room. As he relaxes, casually wander out of sight for short periods. As he improves, you can leave him crated for short periods while you are out of the house.

Why this works: Your dog will view the crate as a safe haven if he's allowed to get accustomed to it gradually. The crate, for him, is like the cave or den he would have found for himself in the wild.

Correcting him when he acts up lets him know that you will not tolerate misbehavior. The incorporation of obedience commands into the crate training teaches self-control; the use of the massage helps the dog calm down.

Prevention: Make sure the crate is big enough for your dog; he should be able to stand up and stretch out in it. Put in some comfortable bedding and some toys. If you are using a wire-mesh crate you can cover most of it with some fabric to make it cozier, but be sure there is good ventilation.

Never put your dog in the crate suddenly and leave him. Always give him time to get used to it.

Never leave your dog in the crate for more than two or three hours at a stretch. It is not fair to crate your dog all day while you are at work. If that is your only option, find your dog another home where he will be able to live uncaged all day.

Once your dog is crate-trained, he will feel safe and secure in strange places where he may need to be crated—at the vet's office, for example, or at a grooming shop or boarding kennel.

Never leave your dog's crate in a drafty place, directly in front of a heater vent, or in bright sunlight.

DEPRESSION

Problem: My dog doesn't seem happy. He mopes around and looks sad and forlorn.

Why your dog is doing that: Your dog may be lonely, or he may not feel well. Perhaps he has just lost a good friend, animal or human, or maybe he senses that you are going away. Aging can also affect his moods and attitude. Whatever the reason for your dog's unhappiness, you can do several things to cheer him up.

What to say and do:

1. Maintain a predictable daily routine. Dogs need consistency to feel safe and happy.

2. Make sure your dog gets adequate daily exercise. Physical movement is uplifting. If he spends a lot of time in his yard, make it entertaining for him by providing a sandbox to dig in, a wading pool on hot summer days, and toys to chew.

3. If he's sad because he lost a doggy friend, try to find other dogs for him to play with—daily, if possible.

4. Playfully review his obedience exercises, but keep the sessions short and upbeat.

5. Include him in your conversations. Talk to him cheerfully.

6. Offer treats and new toys to perk him up.

7. Dogs are affected by their owners' moods. If you are sick, worried, or sad, your dog will sense this.

8. Give your dog lots of companionship. If you are gone all day, take him on outings when you return, and let him sleep in your room. Consider getting another dog as a companion for him.

9. Spend quiet time with him daily, giving him a calming massage.

10. Check with your veterinarian to determine if his depression is physically caused, and make sure he is getting a balanced nutritious diet.

Why this works: It doesn't take much to bring some spark back into your dog's life. A daily routine that includes the activities that your dog loves will provide immediate relief from his depression, and will give him something to look forward to every day.

Prevention: Include your dog in your daily life. As our dogs get older, we sometimes begin to take them for granted. Maybe we skip some of the walks, the park romps, and the visits to friends, and our dogs end up neglected. Be sure to show your dog how much you love him and enjoy his company. And do so every day.

DIGGING

Problem: My dog loves to dig in the yard. He's destroying most of the lawn.

Why your dog is doing this: Dogs dig to make a nest for themselves, to release excess energy, to find cooler ground in the summer, to bury things in the yard, and to investigate intriguing smells and bugs.

What to say and do:

1. Fill each hole almost to the top and then top it off with one of his stools. This should discourage your dog from digging in that place again.

2. If you catch him digging, spray him with water, throw the shaker can at him, or do the scruff grip while telling him firmly, "No! No digging here!" Distract him with a toy. Provide him with a sandbox or acceptable digging area. Take him there and say happily, "You can dig here." Then dig up some dirt or sand yourself to encourage him.

Why this works: If you catch your dog in the act and correct him, or if he is repelled by his own stool, he will think twice about digging in those spots and providing him with an acceptable digging area gives him an outlet for his natural instinct.

Prevention: Provide your dog with a sandbox or a special place where he can dig. Sprinkle some bone meal there, or bury a real bone. A large stump buried in his sandbox will give him hours of fun as he tries to dig it up.

Keep him in his own special yard when you are not home.

Make sure your dog gets plenty of people time. Dogs who are banished to the yard get bored and lonely, and digging is one way for them to entertain themselves.

Make sure your dog gets plenty of exercise, and give him toys to play with and things to gnaw on. If he likes water, give him a plastic wading pool. The more other interesting things he has to entertain him, the less digging he'll do. Secure wire mesh flat on the ground over areas that you want to discourage digging in, or fence those areas.

DIGGING HIS WAY OUT OF THE YARD

Problem: My dog digs his way out of our fenced yard. I'm afraid he's going to get lost or hit by a car.

Why your dog is doing this: Your dog is probably bored with his life in the yard and wants to see what great adventures await him in the world outside.

What to say and do:

1. If you catch your dog digging, or if you see him sniffing at some old escape spot, toss the shaker can at his rump, spritz him with the hose or spray bottle, and shoo him away, speaking firmly.

2. Hide out on the other side of the fence and ambush your dog as he comes through his hole. Toss a bucket of cold water in his face and say, "Hey! Go back! Shame!" Kick the fence (not the dog) a couple of times.

3. Pile his stools along the fence line, especially where he likes to dig.

4. For incorrigible diggers an electric fence wire along the bottom of the fence will discourage them. Pet stores and farm stores sell electric fence kits specifically for dogs. This may sound drastic, but after a couple of zaps your dog will be safe in his yard, and not get killed by a truck in the street. Turn the fence off when the children are outside. After your dog has been zapped a few times, you can keep the fence off.

Why this works: Catching your dog in the act can be somewhat effective, but for dogs that are determined to escape, the only sure bet is the electric fence. But remember, by creating a quality life for your dog you can keep him happy and safe at home.

Prevention: Make sure your dog does not spend his whole life imprisoned in the yard. Give him plenty of exercise, spend quality time with him every day, and practice his obedience training in the yard. Let him stay inside the house with you when you are home and sleep near you at night.

Make his yard fun and entertaining by providing a sandbox, a wading pool, and chew toys. A cozy doghouse will give him a den to retreat to.

Make sure that the bottom of the fence is flush with the ground, and teach your dog when he's young to respect the fence. Don't have your dog with you when you install or fix the fence or fill in the holes. He'll be curious and want to help you out. Don't let your dog jump on the fence or even put his paws on it.

See also:
Roaming
Running away

DOG DOOR, FEAR OF

Problem: My dog won't use the dog door we installed. She barks and backs away from it.

Why your dog is doing this: She is probably afraid of the door and the flap. This new device is foreign to her, and threatening.

What to say and do:

1. Make sure that the door is installed at an accessible height. Your dog should be able to step through without scraping her belly or having to jump. If necessary, build up the floor area on either side of the door to form a ramp.

2. Offer your dog some cheese or liverwurst when she is just inches from the door flap. Then smear some on the flap and encourage her to lick if off. Show her how to push the flap out of the way, and have a helper outside the door to feed her some more treats when she sticks her head through the flap.

3. Toss some food on the other side of the flap and hold the flap open for her. Keep encouraging her with happy words until she steps through the door. Practice until she is comfortable going back and forth.

4. If she is still afraid to go through the door on her own, gently help her through. Praise her and offer her a treat each time.

5. If your dog continues to be spooked, tape the flap securely open with duct tape, let her use it this way for several days, and then try letting the flap down. If she balks, tape the flap back up and tape a piece of cloth over the top half of the opening so she can see through the bottom. Lengthen the cloth as she learns to go in and out. Finally, drop the flap back down.

Why this works: This technique allows your dog to get used to the door gradually.

Prevention: Make sure the dog door is installed at the correct height for your dog. Encourage her to sniff and investigate the door, but don't shove her through. If she is apprehensive, be patient and make sure you don't scare her. If you can, install a door with flexible plastic rather than metal flaps; they are safer.

EATING CAT FOOD AND CAT FECES

Problem: My dog steals the cat's food, and—worse—he eats my kitty's excrement!

Why your dog is doing this: Cat food is very tasty and a real treat to dogs. It is higher in protein than dog food and is more strongly flavored. And, as repulsive as this sounds, cat feces are also a doggie delicacy.

What to say and do:

1. Put your cat's food on a counter, out of your dog's reach, and place the litter box where your dog can't get at it.

2. Give your cats access to a room that's safe from the dog. Wedge the door open just wide enough for your cat, put a cat door in, or install a barrier that your cat can jump over.

3. Place the litter box in a large dog carrier, wedging the door open just enough for your cat. Or buy a cat box with a lid so that the dog can't get into it.

4. Ask your vet to test your dog for parasites, which could contribute to this problem.

Why this works: By removing the temptation, you can guarantee that your dog won't get into trouble.

Prevention: Keep your cat's food and litter box out of the dog's way. Provide your dog with a healthy natural diet; sometimes this problem has a nutritional origin.

Put Tabasco sauce on your cat's feces and ones you find in your yard or on walks, to discourage your dog from eating them. If he keeps encountering cat feces that are too spicy to eat, he may abandon this practice for good—you can only hope.

EATING FECES OF OTHER ANIMALS

Problem: My dog loves to eat excrement from horses, cows, geese, and other animals.

Why your dog is doing this: The manure of grazing animals contains partially digested plants, which domestic dogs crave. In the wild state, dogs got their greens from the contents of the digestive tracts of the herbivorous animals they killed. The average domestic dog's diet doesn't include fresh vegetables, so your dog is getting his greens from the manure.

What to say and do:

1. If you catch your dog in the act, sternly tell him, "Leave it!" If that has no effect, use the spray bottle, shaker can, or scruff grip. Praise him for ignoring the manure; find him something acceptable to play with and put in his mouth.

2. Practice the obedience commands in the barnyard and pastures so he learns to control himself there. If he makes a dive for some manure, give him a leash snap, tell him, "Leave it!" and resume training.

3. Have your dog checked for parasites, which could contribute to this habit.

Why this works: By correcting your dog in the act, you are giving him a clear message that you disapprove of his behavior. By practicing his obedience training around the barnyard, you are teaching him to listen to you in that environment.

Prevention: A healthy diet may solve this problem. Add fresh vegetables—grated carrots, broccoli, parsley, or alfalfa sprouts—to your dog's food.

Fence the pasture and barnyard to keep your dog out of trouble.

EATING GARBAGE

Problem: My dog raids the trash every opportunity he gets.

Why your dog is doing this: Dogs are scavengers. They hung around caves and gnawed on bones and other remains from the humans' meals, much as they now hang around the table, waiting for scraps.

What to say and do:

1. Uncover the garbage can, set it on the floor, and wait in ambush. If your dog sticks his head in it, kick the can (not the dog) so that it jumps up at him, tell him firmly, "Leave it!" and shoo him away. If that doesn't faze him, use the shaker can or spray bottle to get his attention and then firmly lecture him.

2. Caution him firmly if he even glances at the garbage can. Remind him, "Leave it!" If he quickly looks away, praise him calmly.

3. Keep the garbage can out of the dog's reach.

4. Have your dog checked for parasites, which could make him hungrier than he would normally be.

Why this works: Startling him in the act makes the consequences of garbage gutting unpleasant.

Keeping the garbage out of reach prevents any raiding.

Prevention: Outdoor garbage cans must have dogproof lids or be kept out of your dog's reach.

Keep the kitchen garbage in a cupboard or on a high countertop. Do not put food garbage in the wastebasket.

Make sure your dog's diet is healthy. Feed him two meals a day, dividing his morning and evening portions equally.

Obedience training will teach your dog that you are the boss, and he will be more likely to respect your wishes when you correct him.

EATING GRASS

Problem: My dog sometimes eats grass and then throws up.

Why your dog is doing this: It is natural for dogs to graze on grass occasionally. It serves as a tonic that causes the dog to vomit up mucus, nondigestible material, and toxins.

What to say and do:

1. If your dog's behavior is otherwise normal, ignore her when she nibbles grass, but keep her off the rugs when she comes inside. If she starts ingesting large quantities of grass, ask your vet to check for stomach trouble or parasites.

2. Give your dog a healthy diet of natural unprocessed foods and fresh vegetables.

Why this works: Allowing your dog to graze on grass helps her stay healthy.

Providing her with fresh vegetables gives her less reason to graze on grass.

Prevention: It's impossible to prevent your dog from eating grass, but you can provide her with nutritious wheat grass that you cultivate in a garden box. Apartment dogs will appreciate this, and by giving her a patch of grass all her own, you'll make sure she has a safe, healthy supply.

WARNING: Never use chemicals on your lawn, shrubs, trees, or houseplants. Herbicides (weed killers) and chemical fertilizers can cause cancer in dogs.

EATING HIS OWN FECES

Problem: My dog sometimes eats his own feces.

Why your dog is doing this: Puppies that are raised with no toys will often play with and then eat their own feces. Those raised in dirty kennels or in puppy mills get feces on them and must lick themselves to get clean. This diminishes their aversion to their own stool. Puppies that are not fed frequently enough during weaning may get hungry and eat their stool. A nutritional deficiency or food absorption problem may also be a contributing factor.

What to say and do:

1. Ask your vet to test your dog for parasites and to prescribe a nutritional supplement, if necessary.

2. Pick up after your dog as he relieves himself. If he turns around to eat his stool, correct him firmly, shoo him away, and distract him with something else to put in his mouth.

3. Put Tabasco sauce on your dog's stools. Many dogs are repelled by hot pepper sauce.

Why this works: Picking up the stools immediately is the only way to guarantee that he won't eat them.

Prevention: Give your dog a well-balanced diet. Feed pups four meals a day until they are three months old, three meals a day until they are six months old, and two meals a day until they reach one year. If your dog seems hungry, keep feeding him two meals a day after one year.

Obedience training will give your dog confidence, forge a bond between you, and make him take you seriously when you correct him.

EATING OTHER DOGS' FOOD

Problem: My dog gobbles down his own food and then eats my other dogs' food.

Why your dog is doing this: Your dog is asserting his dominance as leader of the pack.

What to say and do:

1. Monitor your dogs at mealtime, or separate them when you feed them.

2. Never put one bowl of food down for each dog and then walk away.

3. Make sure each dog's meal is equally nutritious and tasty, so they don't want some other dog's better-smelling food.

4. Have your veterinarian check your dogs for parasites, which could cause them to be abnormally hungry.

Why this works: By separating the dogs while they eat, and by monitoring their manners, you can stop food-stealing altogether. If you make each dog's meal equally yummy, there will be less incentive to go after another dog's food.

Prevention: Do not put your dogs' food bowls down and walk away. Separate the dogs at mealtime, or stand guard until they are finished.

See also:
Overeating

EATING, PICKY

Problem: My dog has become so fussy about food that I can't seem to please him.

Why your dog is doing this: Your dog has taste buds, just as we do, and he knows what he likes and doesn't like. If you have catered to his tastes, he is probably holding out for his favorite foods.

What to say and do:

1. Give your dog a well-balanced diet, and make sure each meal has the same ingredients and tastes exactly the same. Try this simple, tasty recipe: Mix a good-quality dry food with cottage cheese or canned dog food, and stir in some warm water. Again, make sure that each meal tastes exactly the same.

2. Give him ten minutes to eat in a distraction-free place. If he doesn't eat his food, pick it up and put it in the fridge until next mealtime. Don't be angry with him. Just say, "You're not hungry? Okay, I'll put the food away."

3. At the next mealtime warm up his leftovers to room temperature, add some fresh food, stir in a little warm water, and put the bowl down again. Sometimes it helps to put some of the food on the floor next to his bowl as a starter. Don't feed him from your hand.

4. Repeat this until he gets hungry and decides to eat (it may take several days—don't give in!) When necessary, mix a fresh batch, using the exact same ingredients. Don't add anything to enhance the flavor.

5. Check with the veterinarian if your dog seems to be really off his food. Picky eating could be a symptom of something more serious.

Why this works: Dogs are stubborn, but they are survivors. Your dog is not going to starve himself to death. When he gets hungry, he'll eat. If each meal tastes the same he will eventually give up waiting for goodies and eat what you put in front of him.

Prevention: Pick a healthy diet and stick to it. Don't feed your dog any treats until he has become a reliable, eager eater. Make sure he can't get to the cat food or steal food from the kids. Don't leave his food down all the time; feed him on a regular schedule. Don't get upset with him if he doesn't eat what you put down. Be very matter-of-fact and calm.

EXCITABLE BEHAVIOR

Problem: My dog gets excited over every little thing. He's wearing us out.

Why your dog is doing this: Exuberance is normal in very young dogs, but if your dog is not a puppy, his constant excitement is not natural. Maybe he does not get enough exercise, or perhaps he spends too much time alone and is starved for companionship. He may also be picking up the nervousness of the people around him, or he could be allergic to something in his diet.

What to say and do:

1. Spend at least twenty minutes of quiet time with your dog every day in a distraction-free place, giving him a massage and settling him down.

2. Obedience-train him, so that he learns to control his body. Mix the training with play and calming massage. Practice lots of down-stays, lengthening the time as he improves.

3. Be sure your dog gets plenty of daily exercise. If possible, let him cut loose off-leash in a safe place, such as a fenced tennis court. If that's impossible, exercise him on a long line. On days when you can't take him out, play with him at home.

4. Make his yard entertaining, and play with him there. Give him a sandbox, a wading pool, and toys to play with and gnaw on.

5. When he gets wild correct him with the leash snap, make him sit, and then settle him down with the calming massage.

6. Make sure your dog's diet—including treats and rawhide chews, which can be processed in formaldehyde and other chemicals—is free of artificial flavoring, food coloring, preservatives, and sweeteners. Just as some people can become agitated from too much caffeine or sugar, dogs can react to certain ingredients by becoming hyperactive.

7. Find a compatible doggy playmate for your dog to be wild with, while you watch him get tired out!

8. If he is a male, have him neutered. This should calm him down. It is a good idea to have your pets neutered anyway. Keeping the canine population down will help to eliminate the need to put millions of dogs to death each year.

Why this works: By providing adequate diet, exercise, obedience training, quiet time, and socializing, you will make your dog mellower and more contented. The obedience training and the calming massage will help your dog settle down.

Prevention: Make sure your dog is not spending his entire life confined in your yard or your house. Let your dog sleep indoors at night, preferably near you.

Make sure your dog's needs are met and that you are calm when you're around him, so you can transmit a calm feeling to him.

See also:
Hyperactivity
Wild behavior in the house
Zooming

FEARFUL URINATING. SEE URINATING WHEN REPRIMANDED

FEAR OF BEING ALONE. SEE AFRAID TO BE ALONE

FEAR OF CERTAIN OBJECTS

Problem: My dog is afraid of certain things—the vacuum cleaner, the mailbox, and the broom, for example.

Why your dog is doing this: Objects that make loud noises or look strange to your dog may startle him, especially if he has had a bad experience with them. Did he ever get hit by a ball? A broom? Get sucked in by the vacuum? If your dog was raised in isolated conditions—a puppy mill, a pet store, or an inhumane kennel, for instance—he could be frightened by noises, objects, or activities that seem common to us.

He may also associate a certain object with abuse. For example, if he was frightened by someone who wore a hat, or hit him with a hat, he could be scared of hats or of people wearing hats. Brooms may frighten him if he was threatened or beaten with them.

What to say and do:

1. Teach or review the obedience commands. Practice near the objects that scare him, but stay far enough away from them so that your dog will feel safe. Move closer to the scary thing as your dog gains confidence. Let him sniff it if he wants to, while you praise him.

2. When your dog seems relaxed, ask a friend to use one of the objects while you are a distance away. Have your friend open and shut the mailbox, turn the vacuum on and off, rattle a trash can, smack a hat gently against his own leg, or move the broom around on the floor, depending on your dog's phobia.

3. Keep up a happy chatter with your dog. If he starts barking, correct him, resuming your praise as soon as he is quiet. Gradually work your way closer to the object as your dog begins to relax. Don't rush! A lack of patience here can unravel progress quickly.

4. Feed your dog or put treats near the things he's afraid of.

5. Remember, a dog's hearing is much keener than a human's. Some high-pitched noises can even hurt his ears. It's natural for him to want to avoid loud or high noises or to respond to them by barking. Allow him space to maneuver out of the way of such noises.

Why this works: This step-by-step approach gives your dog a chance to acquaint himself gradually with the things that scare him. By practicing his obedience work around the scary objects, you will increase his confidence and reduce his fears.

Prevention: Never scare or tease your dog with household objects. Make certain that things are secure in their place so they do not fall over and frighten him. Don't let children or friends tease or spook your dog. Socialize young dogs daily. If your dog shies away from something while on a walk, pause and encourage him to sniff and investigate it. Always speak to him in an upbeat, reassuring voice.

See also:
Abused dog
Nervousness
Noises, fear of

FEAR OF OTHER DOGS

Problem: Whenever my dog sees another dog, she hides behind me and trembles. If she's loose with me in the park, she'll run for cover.

Why your dog is doing this: Your dog finds other dogs intimidating and is clinging to you for security. If she hasn't been socialized enough she doesn't know how to interact with other dogs or how to interpret their language. Dogs bred in puppy mills and raised in individual cages in pet stores (an unforgivably cruel way to breed and keep puppies) often don't know how to interact because they have had no contact with other dogs and they lack doggy social skills. Since you are your dog's pack family, she runs to you for security.

What to say and do:

1. When another dog approaches, talk to your dog in a very happy, inviting voice, and speak to the other dog in the same friendly, happy voice. You want your dog to see that you are relaxed and welcoming toward the other dog.

2. Do not reassure your dog in a worried tone of voice, or your dog will think something is wrong. Do not touch or pet your dog, or she'll discover that acting scared gets coddling from you.

3. Is she is on-leash, keep the leash loose. If she wants to roll on her back, or squat and pee, that's fine—she's showing submission. Once she sees that she won't be hurt, she'll relax a bit. If she snaps at the other dog for sniffing her too closely, that's okay too. She is justified in setting some limits, even when she's being submissive.

4. Find her a suitable doggy playmate, one who is gentle, submissive, and preferably smaller. Introduce them on neutral territory or in a spacious fenced yard and have both dogs off-leash. Give the dogs a half hour or more to become acquainted and play. If your dog runs over to you for protection, talk happily to her and then ignore her. Have toys available for the dogs to play with and water for them to drink.

5. If off-leash romps are impossible, take her for an on-leash walk with another friendly dog and its owner. This will help her view the other dog as a possible friend she's out on the trail with, exploring new territory.

Why this works: Creating a relaxed, upbeat mood around other dogs will help your dog relax. Finding a regular playmate who is smaller, friendly, and gentle will help her to overcome her fears and learn to make friends. Once she has made one doggy friend, she will view other dogs as potential friends, too.

Prevention: Play with your dog when she first notices a dog at a distance. Speak happily and feed her some treats. Carry a favorite squeaky toy or ball and have a little game. If you make sure she's having fun when other dogs go by, she'll associate seeing other dogs with having a good time.

See also:
Shyness

FIGHTING WITH OTHER DOGS

Problem: My dog gets into fights on a regular basis. I'm afraid someone—pup or person—is going to get hurt.

Why your dog is doing this: Dogs fight to establish dominance, and if two dogs are equally matched in size and determination, the fights can be very nasty and dangerous. If the dogs are not equally matched, and one is more submissive than the other, dominance may be established quickly and the fight will end.

Fighting with strange dogs and fighting among your own dogs must be dealt with in different ways.

FIGHTING WITH STRANGE DOGS

What to say and do:

1. Have your male dog neutered. Sometimes this will settle a dog down and make him less aggressive.

2. Obedience training is an absolute must for aggressive dogs. It may allow you to control your dog and prevent a fight by putting him in a down-stay, although this level of control takes a lot of training.

3. Carry a spray bottle with you on walks. The instant your dog sees another dog and tenses up (watch his ears and tail), spray him liberally, snap the leash, tell him, "Leave it!" Get his attention and then praise him. Have him sit, and calm him with the massage. Alternate between the correction, obedience work, and calming massage as necessary.

4. An alternative to the correction-and-control approach is to talk happily to your dog when he sees another dog. If the other dog comes up to you, leave your leash loose, stand back, and let the dogs sniff each other. When they are done checking each other out, casually call your dog away.

5. When young male dogs are growing up, they often act obnoxious around female dogs. The female dogs will clearly tell them to back off, but the males may be undaunted and may sass back at the female. A small spat could ensue. Once young males learn that females will always have the last word on sexual matters, this type of fighting comes to an end. (Sound familiar?)

FIGHTING AMONG YOUR OWN DOGS

What to say and do:

1. Let your dogs establish their pecking order without your interference, especially if they are young or new to each other. Just make sure nobody gets hurt.

2. If they get too aggressive with each other, you must forbid any aggressive behavior by establishing yourself as the pack leader. This takes obedience training for all of your dogs and strong corrections for any show of aggression. Don't wait for a fight; correct them for growling or posturing. Use the spray bottle to interrupt them. Then put them in the down-stay near each other.

3. If your dogs fight continually, you will need to keep them separated or find a home for one of them.

4. Routinely practice obedience training with your dogs. Have them do sit-stays and long down-stays side by side. Let them know they can be next to each other respectfully and that you are the ultimate authority.

5. If your dogs get testy at mealtime, feed them in separate places so as not to trigger possessiveness over food. If they growl or scrap over a resting spot, provide two cozy beds and teach each dog to go to his own bed. If they tend to fight over who gets petted, make both dogs sit and stay, respectfully, before you pet the one you want.

Why this works: Obedience training teaches self-control and establishes you as the top dog. The calming massage helps you settle your dog when he is tense. Neutering helps prevent aggression, and socializing teaches young dogs how to interpret other dogs' signals and how to play with them.

Prevention: Socializing young dogs in free play will help prevent them from growing up into fighters. They may still do some posturing for dominance and even have a few words, but full-blown fights will be less likely.

The best prevention for fighting in male dogs is neutering at a young age, before they start lifting their leg to mark territory or showing any aggressive behavior. Intact males will often regard neutered males as females of some sort, so when a neutered male warns away an intact male dog he is usually respected.

Obedience training teaches your dog that you are the pack leader and you won't tolerate any fighting in your pack. Enroll your dog in an obedience class so that he learns self-control around other dogs.

Spend twenty minutes a day doing calming message work to relax your dog so you will be able to calm him when he is around the other dogs.

WARNING: If you have a confirmed nasty fighter, keep him away from the other dogs and get professional help.

GROWLING AT YOU

Problem: My dog growls at us when we try to make him do something he doesn't want to do.

Why your dog is doing this: Your dog's own personality and the way you raise him will determine how he sees himself in relation to the rest of the pack. If he feels that he's at the bottom of the pecking order he will be submissive and eager to please you. If he thinks he's at the top, he will resist you and will growl, snarl, snap, or bite to force you to back off.

What to say and do:

1. *Get professional help.* A dog who growls and challenges his human is a dog who might bite. It takes the knowledge and skillful handling of a trainer or behaviorist to read your dog correctly and determine the best way to deal with him. All dogs are different and need to be handled differently. Some growling problems are not as serious as others and can be corrected relatively easily, while others might reflect a serious and determined mind-set that may be totally resistant to change. Only a knowledgeable dog handler can determine that.

2. Teach your dog some simple obedience commands in an upbeat way. Keep the lessons short, and play with him before and after each session. If your dog growls at you during a training session, stop, and get professional help.

3. Be less affectionate with your dog. Dish out warm praise only after he has followed a simple command such as a twenty-second sit-stay. Your dog must earn your affection.

4. If your dog is being stubborn, distract him with something fun. If you tell him to get off the couch and he growls at you, lure him off the couch with a toy or a game.

5. Leave a leash on your dog when you are at home to make him easier to catch and control. Use your obedience commands, leash in hand, when you need your dog to listen to you. Praise him lavishly for cooperating. For this purpose, attach the leash to his buckle collar, not to a choke chain, and do not use a leash with a loop handle that could catch on things.

6. Keep your dog off your bed and all other furniture. Give him a cozy bed of his own on the floor.

7. If you have been leaving food out for your dog all the time, stop doing so. Feed him regular meals instead.

8. Spend a half hour a day giving your dog a slow calming massage in a distraction-free place. If he doesn't want to sit still for half an hour, put him in a shorter sit-stay and gradually build up to thirty minutes.

Why this works: Changing your dog's routine will help him see you as his boss instead of his personal servant.

Obedience training will also change your dog's mind about his exalted status in the pack as he learns to enjoy being submissive and to let you control him.

By distracting him with a treat or the prospect of a walk in situations that usually set him off, you will change his mood from grumpy to happy, and this may prevent a confrontation and bite from occurring.

Prevention: To prevent a dog from becoming the pack leader, you must show him from the start that you are the undisputed leader of the pack. Let him know this in language he can understand, through continual obedience-training sessions.

Neutering male dogs before they mature sexually and start leg lifting (when they're six to seven months old) will help prevent them from becoming aggressive and dominant. This is not a replacement for obedience training, however.

Crate-training your dog at a young age teaches him that he has his own designated place in the household.

Keeping your dog off your bed and furniture will keep him beneath you, on the floor, which translates to below you in status.

WARNING: If your dog continues to growl at you, don't mess around. Get professional help.

See also:
Crate training

GUESTS, PESTERING

Problem: My dog constantly pesters visitors for attention.

Why your dog is doing this: Your dog loves attention and knows that your guests don't know how to send him away, which makes them prime targets for petting and playing.

What to say and do:

1. Practice some obedience training indoors with your dog. When he improves, invite your friends over and train him with them there.

2. Let him greet your friends and visit a bit. Then put him in a down-stay at your feet. Keep him on a leash if necessary. Give him something to chew and make him stay put. If he's restless, give him a blanket to lie on.

3. Teach him to go to his bed and lie down. If he bugs your guest, shoo him away or use the leash to lead him to his bed. Be firm with him, but remember to praise him for cooperating.

4. When he is well-mannered on-leash, let him wander around, dragging the leash. If he starts to bother anyone, correct him and send him away. As he improves, remove the leash but keep a close watch on him.

Why this works: Your dog will learn that he can survive even if he's not the center of attention. By practicing his obedience training in your living room, you give him a chance to learn gradually and naturally to control himself around your guests.

Prevention: Although it's cute to watch your dog place his favorite squeeze toy on your friend's lap, don't laugh at him. You can't expect your friends to know how to send him away, so that task is up to you.

Practice long down-stays with the dog on-leash at your feet. This will teach him not to bother you when you are alone with him.

See also:
Begging at mealtime
Crate training

HAND-SHYNESS

Problem: My dog seems to be afraid of my hands. When I reach out to pet her, she sometimes shies away.

Why your dog is doing this: Your dog has had a bad experience with human hands. If she was ever grabbed at while on the loose—even if she wasn't corrected, just nabbed—she has learned that hands curtail fun. If she was abused in any way, she will naturally be afraid of any hands that reach out toward her.

What to say and do:

1. When you reach out to pet her, move your hands slowly and always stroke her under her chin first. Avoid downward sweeping arm motions by keeping your arms low and your hands in sight. Talk to her in sweet tones, and squat down to her level.

2. Teach her some obedience commands, including the sit-stay. When she is able to do a sit-stay for three minutes at the end of a 6-foot leash, put her in a sit-stay, go to the end of the leash, and hold the leash in your left hand. Approach her, remind her to stay, and give her the hand signal with your right hand about a foot from her face. Pause, then stroke her slowly several times with the same hand. Pause again, repeat the stay command and hand signal, and back out to the end of the leash. Repeat this sequence several times, approaching her from different angles. End the stay by releasing her with a happy "Okay!" when you are about 3 feet from her. Squat down to greet and praise her as she comes to you.

3. Spend a minimum of twenty minutes a day giving her a calming massage. Work especially on her neck and collar area, so that she views your touch as pleasant. Whenever you praise her for a correct response, stroke her gently at the same time.

Why this works: If you consistently handle your dog gently she will learn to trust your touch. Because she knows she can trust you in the sit-stay, she can control her fears, sit still, and let you touch her. The more frequently she experiences your pleasant, deliberate touch, the more trusting she'll become. The daily massage sessions will help her to relax under your hands.

Prevention: Never grab at your dog or correct her with the scruff grip. This will only make her more shy; if she gets really scared, she may snap at you. Leave a leash on her in the house that you can pick up so you won't have to grab at her. Correct her verbally or use the spray bottle or shaker can rather than a hands-on correction. If you have a small dog, don't abruptly snatch her up; gently put your hands around her when she's on the floor, stroke her slowly, and quietly pick her up.

Instruct your friends and family in how to handle her. If you see that they are handling her incorrectly, don't hesitate to correct them.

See also:
Abused dog
Hard to catch

Happy Piddling. see Urinating, Involuntary

Hard to Catch

Problem: When my dog gets loose, he's really hard to catch. He plays keep-away.

Why your dog is doing this: Your dog stays out of reach because getting caught means the end of his fun. He's also worried about what you might do to him when you do catch him.

What to say and do:

1. Obedience training is the first step to teaching your dog to listen to you and respect you.

2. Don't chase him and then lunge and make a grab for him. That will make him harder to catch the next time. Instead, walk or run away from him, calling to him, "Come on, let's go!" When he gets near you, sit down or lie down on the ground and pretend you have found something intriguing. Dig in the grass and pretend to be eating something. In short, act silly.

3. If he comes close enough, take hold of him gently (don't grab), and scratch him in all his favorite places. Put his leash on, play with him, and pop him a few treats. Make it fun for him to come to you—even if you feel like screaming at him!

4. If he refuses to return to you, ask a neighbor or friend to help you catch him, or try to lure him back with another dog. If you get in your car, he may come running to get in so as not to be left behind. Sometimes propping the front door open and ignoring him will give him a way back in the house.

5. Don't correct him when you get him, even if you are angry. This will just reinforce in his mind the idea that coming to you is unpleasant. Review some of his obedience training; remind him what "come" means. Give him lots of praise, but make him pay close attention to you.

Why this works: If your dog discovers that when he does come, you are fun and not angry, he'll make himself easier to catch. A firm foundation in obedience training reinforces your position as the boss.

Prevention: Teach your dog to stay and to come. Often, before your dog will actually respond to the come command, you will be able to give him the stay command and the hand signal, and he'll freeze and let you come up to him. Praise him lavishly if he does this—even if you've just spend the last half hour trying to catch him. Practice his training in your front yard and on the sidewalk. Don't grab your dog and drag him disgustedly back into the house. If you find it impossible to be civil with him, channel your anger into some firm-but-fair obedience routines and end on a friendly note.

Don't play chase games with him in the house or yard, even if he loves them. Teach him to retrieve his toys and bring them back to you.

Give your dog plenty of daily exercise. Romps in the park or play sessions with other dogs will tire him out and reduce his need to run circles around you.

Make sure your dog is not spending his entire life confined to your yard or house. If he must often be confined, make sure he has toys, a sandbox, and a wading pool. Let him sleep near you at night.

Having him off-leash as much as possible in safe places will make freedom seem less precious to him.

See also:
Hand-shy
Off-leash misbehavior
Roaming
Running away

HEAT, FEMALE

Problem: My female dog will be in heat soon. She's beginning to behave differently and isn't listening as well as usual.

Why your dog is doing this: Your dog is distracted by the call of Mother Nature. She is focused on the smells of other dogs and on leaving her own scent (urine) everywhere.

What to say and do:

1. Have your dog spayed before she's nine months old. Spaying a dog when she's in heat is risky, so be sure to wait until she's well out. Spaying will prevent her from getting pregnant and having puppies that may never have permanent homes. It will also help reduce the huge number of homeless dogs who fill our dog pounds and shelters and whose fate is death.

2. Don't walk your dog in your neighborhood when she's in heat or close to it. She will attract every male in the area. Try to limit her urinating to your backyard or, better yet, drive her to an empty field where she can relieve herself and get some exercise—but be careful.

3. Watch her closely, since she may sneak off as soon as you aren't watching her. Don't let her out in your yard without supervision, even if the yard is fenced. You never know what clever male has found his way in. Always keep a flashlight on her at night or have your yard well lighted.

4. When you must leave her alone, do not leave her in your yard. Keep her indoors, crated if necessary, and instruct anyone dealing with her to be totally vigilant about this.

5. If you have other female dogs in your house, fights may break out between normally friendly dogs. If that is the case, have them together only under supervision.

6. If you have an unneutered male dog in the same household, be prepared for him to whine or howl for the duration of the bitch's heat (three weeks); he might also begin to lift his leg indoors to show his dominance and to mark his territory. So that both dogs can continue to enjoy house time, yard time, and people time, use the crate to confine one dog while the other dog is in the house or the yard. Then confine the other dog to the crate while the first one is free. Rotate them methodically from one location to the other. Don't leave the bitch in heat with an unneutered male dog for even a few seconds, no matter how old or tiny he may seem compared to the female. Remember, boys will be boys!

7. The heat cycle is three weeks long, and your dog will bleed the entire time. She will be fertile generally between the tenth day and the sixteenth. She will be distracted and restless for the entire cycle, and she'll attract males the whole time.

8. If, despite your precautions, you find her in the process of mating, *don't try to pull the dogs apart.* Dogs form a physical tie during the breeding process that can last up to forty-five minutes. If you try to pull them apart, *you could injure them badly.* Simply keep them still and calm and wait it out. Then take your bitch to the vet for a shot to abort the litter. This shot, unfortunately, will bring your dog back into heat again for another full three weeks, but there will be no puppies.

Why this works: You must be extremely careful with a bitch in heat. Keeping your female under close supervision at all times and exercising her away from your home will keep the roaming males from finding her easily. But find her they will, which is why you must observe your dog whenever she's in your yard. At night, always use a flashlight for potty runs, and never leave her outside all night when she's in season.

Prevention: Have your female spayed before her first heat. If she is already between heat cycles, have her spayed now. Unless you are a serious breeder with top-quality dogs, lots of time and money, and good homes already lined up for your pups, do not breed your dog. The animal shelters are overflowing with unwanted dogs, all of which began as someone's litter of puppies. Spaying also reduces the chances that your dog will get mammary or uterine tumors, which can be fatal.

HEAT, MALE

Problem: My male dog lifts his leg on everything and pays little attention to us. He's pushy with other dogs, male and female, and other dogs snap at him.

Why your dog is doing this: Unneutered (intact) males are always in heat, so to speak—this means they are always ready to breed. To display his maleness, your dog marks his territory by urinating.

What to say and do:

1. Get your dog neutered. Neutering will also prevent testicular and prostate cancer as well as tumors or hernias around the anus. Intact male dogs tend to be much more aggressive to other male dogs and can get into frequent fights. Neutering will curb or prevent this problem if done before fighting habits start. Intact males tend to roam more and can disappear for days when a female is in heat in the neighborhood. They may take up residence outside your poor neighbors' door for the three weeks their female is in heat. Intact males also are more likely to urinate in your house, repeatedly marking several chosen spots to freshen up their scent posts and claim the territory as theirs.

2. Obedience training is imperative for intact males, as they tend to be more dominant with their family. Practice indoors to remind your dog that he must respect you and your house.

Why this works: Unneutered male dogs that are obedience-trained from a young age will grow up respectful of your home and be less likely to mark indoors. Practicing obedience lessons inside reminds your dog that you are the pack leader and that he must respect your space.

Prevention: The only way to prevent your male dog from roaming, marking territory, and fighting with other dogs is to get him neutered or keep him in a fenced yard.

Short of neutering, don't let your dog drag you to every bush so he can urinate on it. Let him mark a couple of bushes on the edge of your property. After that, you choose where he gets to mark on the walk—just a few bladder-emptying pees will do.

If you must keep your dog intact, make sure to socialize him around other friendly dogs as he grows up, so that he will learn how to interact.

Start obedience training when your dog is young, with puppy kindergarten, and carry on with the training through adolescence and into adulthood.

Make sure he has a spacious, securely fenced yard.

See also:
Humping
Urinating to mark territory

HOUSEBREAKING

Problem: My dog doesn't have a clue about where he is supposed to relieve himself. He just doesn't get it. He goes all over the house, even on the rugs.

Why your dog is doing this: Dogs who have never been taught where to relieve themselves are really at a loss about what's expected of them. Usually they will look for any absorbent surface that is out of the way.

What to say and do: A thorough housebreaking program is prevention-oriented. It consists of scheduled confinement, regular potty runs, monitored house time, regular meals, good health, obedience training, and proper handling of mistakes. The following rules will help you housebreak your dog.

CONFINEMENT

1. Until your dog is housebroken, he cannot be allowed to roam around the house unmonitored. When you're with him, you can tether him to his bed area or to you. Just be sure he doesn't tangle himself in his leash. If he is crate trained, use the crate for his naps, when it is too chaotic in your house to keep track of him, when you leave the house for three hours or less, or when you are sleeping, on the phone, or in the shower.

2. If you must leave him for longer than three hours and you can't leave him outside, arrange for someone to come and let him out of his crate at two- to three-hour intervals for a half-hour potty run and leg stretch. If this is impossible, set up a pen for him in the house, basement, or garage. Give him toys and a cozy bed. Provide a designated potty area by covering the remainder of the floor with newspapers or by giving him a potty box filled with wood chips, shavings, dirt, grass (from rolls of sod), or some combination thereof. The box can be framed with two-by-fours and set on an old piece of linoleum.

3. When he's used to being confined for two-hour stretches, let him sleep overnight next to your bed in his crate or safely tether him and provide him with a very cozy bed that he won't want to leave. If he is under fifteen weeks old, he won't be able to wait all night and you will have to let him out when he gets restless, or leave him in his pen.

POTTY RUNS

1. Immediately after every meal, nap, night's sleep, and whenever you return home, take your dog directly outside. Don't carry him; let him follow you. Rattle the doorknob, saying happily, "Do you want to go outside?" If he has been left outside, don't bring him in immediately. Spend some time with him outdoors and bring him in after he urinates. Take him to the same potty area every time. If your yard is not fenced, use an 8- to 10-foot leash, as some dogs need a little distance from you.

2. Talk encouragingly to him, but wait until he finishes before your praise him. If you praise him too soon, he may cut it short and finish inside. Some dogs poop twice in a row; if this is his style, give him extra time.

HOUSE TIME

1. If he does relieve himself outside, bring him back indoors, but don't give him the run of the house. Let him roam free in the room you are hanging out in, and keep an eye on him.

2. If he doesn't relieve himself outside (because it's raining or he got distracted by something), confine him immediately as soon as you bring him back indoors, but don't be angry with him. Try again fifteen to twenty minutes later. Take him back outside and repeat the potty run. Eventually he will learn what the trips outside are for, and he'll wait until he's outside to relieve himself.

3. Introduce him to the rest of the house slowly, room by room, under supervision and only after he has just relieved himself outside. Be involved with him—play with him, practice his obedience training, let him take naps at your feet. This will help him view those rooms as his living space, and he'll want to keep them clean. If he has a particular spot he likes to mess in, train him there (long down-stays work well), or put his bed there, since dogs won't mess where they sleep.

MISTAKES

1. If you catch your dog relieving himself in the house, interrupt him gently, say, "Let's go outside," and take him outside. Don't be harsh or he will become afraid of your hands and approach and will sneak off to relieve himself.

2. If you find a pile or puddle after the fact, don't drag him back to the mess and correct him. Instead, casually wait for him to walk past the mess and acknowledge it himself, even with the slightest glance or sniff. Growl at him: "Shame on you!" Then clean up the mess with a product that will take the smell out.

Why this works: Limiting your dog's access in the house when he can't be closely watched will prevent him from relieving himself inside. Escorting him outside allows you to monitor him and praise him for cooperating. By keeping close track of his elimination times, you learn when it is safe to give him free time in the house. Since housebreaking is a habit, if your dog has no choice but to relieve himself outside he will develop the habit of going outside and will wait to do so.

FOOD AND WATER

F eed your dog regularly scheduled meals; don't leave his food down all the time. What goes in on schedule will generally come out on schedule. If your dog is six months old, he should be on two meals a day, which you can reduce to one meal a day when he is a year old, if you prefer. Puppies from three to six months need three meals a day; puppies under three months need four meals a day. Put the food down, give him ten minutes to eat it, then pick it up. Feed him a high-quality natural food so there will be less bulk and less stool. If you must give him treats between meals, they should be high quality and given in tiny amounts; freeze-dried or baked liver (available in pet stores) make an excellent treat. During the night give him no access to water, and let him have his last drink two hours before his last potty run. Take him outside just before you go to bed even if you have to wake him up to do so. Do let him have access to water during the day. It is not fair to withhold water from dogs during the day, except when they are in their crates.

Don't give him lots of rawhide chewies if he chomps them right down. They will make him very thirsty, and he will drink more and urinate more. They are also hard to digest and produce extra stool. Some rawhide is processed in formaldehyde and is not healthy for your dog, so check with your pet supply store before purchasing any.

Make sure he's not getting extra food by stealing the cat's food, getting into garbage, eating the neighbor's pets' food, or being given leftovers. This will make him harder to housebreak.

SIGNALS

W atch your dog very closely when he's loose in the house. If you see him glance at the door, act fast and say, "Let's go outside! Good boy!"

If your dog stops what he is doing and looks distracted, starts sniffing around, or wanders toward an area where he has had accidents, quickly encourage him to follow you outside. Remember not to carry him—let him walk.

OBEDIENCE TRAINING

P utting him through an obedience program will elevate you to pack leader. Practice the training indoors so he will view the house as an area in which he must respect you. Obedience training will also help you and your dog work together as a team and feel good about each other.

HEALTH

M ake sure your dog is free of internal and external parasites and infections, especially those of the urinary tract. A constant need to urinate could be caused by an infection or other medical problem. Schedule regular veterinary checkups.

NEUTERING

H ave your male dog neutered, especially if he is lifting his leg in your house. It's more than likely he's marking territory. If your dog is six months or older, talk with your veterinarian immediately about getting him sterilized.

PUPPIES

P uppies need access to a potty area during the night. They cannot be expected to wait all night until they are fourteen to sixteen weeks old, since they simply do not have the necessary muscle control. Until then, have them spend the night in a pen in which you have arranged a cozy bed such as a crate with the door propped open. This pen should also have a potty area. Cover the remainder of the floor with newspapers or make a natural potty box out of two-by-fours and fill it with sod, wood chips, shavings, soil, or a combination. You can also crate your puppy next to your bed once he's crate-trained, but be prepared to take him out whenever he fusses. (You'll find this gets very tiring after a few nights.)

During the day, puppies from about seven to twelve weeks old are best confined in a pen rather than in a crate when you're not there to supervise them. If you have a secure puppy pen outside with some shade, and if the weather is mild, you can leave him outdoors. Make sure the pen is safe from predators, both human and animal (raccoons, large birds of prey, other dogs, and so on). Never leave any pup crated for more than two hours at a stretch. It's unfair to confine your dog to a crate all day long. It will cause them to feel abandoned and scared as well as lonely and miserable. If they are crated too long, they are often forced to mess in their bed, which is totally contrary to their instinct to keep their nest clean. This can make them very difficult to housebreak. If you feel you have no alternative to keeping you puppy crated all day, you should find another home for him where he won't have to grow up in a cage.

Ideally, the indoor pen should be situated adjacent to the door to his fenced outside potty area so the puppy will relieve himself on the papers near the door. When you are home, leave the pen door and house door open, so the pup can go freely from his pen to a securely fenced area outside.

See also:
Crate training

HOUSEBREAKING: PAPER TRAINING

Problem: I am trying to paper-train my dog, since I can't always take her outside, but she doesn't seem to be catching on.

Why your dog is doing this: If your dog has to relieve herself and isn't in the habit of using the papers, she will seek other absorbent areas.

What to say and do:

CONFINEMENT

1. Don't let your dog roam around the house unmonitored, even for just a few minutes. If you can't watch her, or if you must leave her home alone, confine her to a pen and cover the entire floor of the pen with newspapers. After she's been using the newspapers for a while, you can slowly reduce the size of the papered area until there is only a small area left. A kitchen, bathroom, porch, or hallway can serve as a pen, as long as it's not isolated. Use a baby gate so she can see outside her area. Wherever you confine her is where she will return to, once she is paper-trained. Put her bed, a water bowl, and some toys in the pen. This is your dog's personal living space. If you also intend to take your dog outdoors to relieve herself, set up the pen adjacent to the door that leads to her outside potty area.

2. You can also crate-train your dog and confine her in the crate when you can't watch for her short periods, to a maximum of two hours during the day. After fourteen weeks of age, she can sleep in the crate overnight in your room with you.

POTTY TIME

1. She will need to relieve herself after every meal, first thing in the morning, and when she wakes up from a nap (especially when she is a puppy), so be sure that you put her in her pen after she eats and when she wakes up. Try to have her walk to the pen rather than be carried, so she'll learn to go there herself. Talk to her on the way: "Let's go potty. Let's go find the papers." Don't hover over her when she's in the pen.

2. Keep her confined until she relieves herself on the papers. Praise her and let her come out for some house time. Keep the pen door open so she will have access to the papers whenever she needs to use them.

House Time

1. Let your dog run loose in the house only after she has relieved herself. Slowly increase her access room by room, starting with the one closest to her papers.

2. Be involved with her when she is loose in the rooms. Practice her obedience lessons, play with her, and let her take naps at your feet (on-leash, so she can't wake up, wander off, and urinate).

Mistakes

1. If you catch her messing in the wrong place, don't be harsh with her. Interrupt her gently and tell her, "No, not here. Let's go to the papers," and encourage her to follow you to her potty area. Confine her and watch her, ready to praise her after she relieves herself.

2. If you find a mess after the fact, don't drag your puppy or dog back to the mess and correct her. Wait until she ambles back over to sniff her mess, and then growl at her: "Shame on you!" Shoo her away and clean up the mess with a solution that will eliminate the smell.

Why this works: Using the papers will become a habit. Whatever surface she finds under her feet when she relieves herself is the area she'll continue to seek out. Limiting her to papers for an extended period of time and letting her have access to the rest of the house only after she's used the papers will get her in the habit of seeking out her papers when she needs to relieve herself. Paper-training is also useful as a backup for times when you can't take your dog out, such as late at night.

Prevention: Feed your dog regular meals. What goes in regularly will come out regularly. Feed her a healthy, high-quality dog food because there is less bulk and hence less stool. Do not leave the food down all the time. Give her ten minutes to eat; then pick up her bowl. Don't give your dog lots of rawhide or salty, artificially flavored treats. They will make her very thirsty, and she'll drink more and thus piddle more often. Rawhide causes more stool and can be hard to digest. Some rawhide is processed in formaldehyde, which is not healthy for your dog.

If your dog is sleeping in a crate at night, withhold water two hours before bedtime. Take her to her potty area just before you go to bed, even if you have to wake her up.

If you see your dog sniffing around the house, have her follow you to the papers, saying, "Let's go to the potty area—good girl!" Keep her confined there until she goes, then praise her and let her out.

Teach your dog some obedience commands and practice them in the house. This will teach your dog to respect you and regard your house as an area where she needs to exhibit some self-control.

Make sure your dog is free of parasites and doesn't have any infections—especially urinary. Get your male dog neutered, since intact males will mark their territory in the house regularly to freshen up their spots. Neutering will take away the urge to do this.

See also:
Crate training

HOUSEBREAKING: SNEAKING AWAY TO RELIEVE HERSELF INDOORS

Problem: My dog won't relieve herself during our long walks, but she sneaks off to relieve herself in the house when nobody is watching. Five minutes after I come back inside I find a puddle on the floor.

Why your dog is doing this: Your dog is afraid to relieve herself in your presence because at some point you or someone else was too harsh on her when you caught her messing in the house. She is now sure that if you see her relieve herself, you'll yell at her, so she won't go while you're outside watching her. She comes back inside and sneaks away.

What to say and do:

1. Don't let your dog roam around freely. Limit her access in the house either by using a crate or keeping her with you with a leash.

2. Take your dog outside periodically for potty runs, talking very positively: "Come on, let's go outside and go potty!" emphasizing the word "outside." Rattle the doorknob happily, making it an exciting moment for your dog.

3. Walk her around on a 10-foot leash—long enough so that you're not hovering over her. Speak softly and encouragingly: "Go potty!" When she finishes, praise her happily: "Good girl! Good to go potty!" Let her know you are very pleased.

4. If your dog does not relieve herself outside, confine her when you return inside and keep her confined until her next potty run—a half hour later for an adult dog, fifteen minutes for a puppy. Keep up this pattern until your dog learns to relieve herself outdoors. Then she can roam around the house for a while, but keep an eye on her.

5. Crate your dog at night so she can't sneak off and relieve herself. Remove her water two hours before her last potty run.

6. Crate her for short periods (up to three hours) during the day if you must be gone. Make sure she relieves herself before you put her in her crate.

Why this works: Dogs will do anything to avoid messing their nest. By keeping her on-leash with you or by confining her to a crate, you are forcing her to hold it in until given the chance to go elsewhere. When you praise her lavishly, her fear about relieving herself in front of you lessens, and her routine will change to wanting to go outside, because she now knows this pleases you.

Prevention: Don't be harsh when you dog messes in the house. Just interrupt her gently and take her outside. Remember to anticipate her potty times and feed her on a regular schedule. If she is young, don't leave her in the house for long periods without a dog door or some way to get outside.

See also:
Crate training

HOWLING

Problem: My dog howls playfully sometimes. Other times he sounds as if it's the end of the world.

Why your dog is doing this: If your dog is howling plaintively, he's telling you he's miserable, in the hope that you'll come and keep him company. If he sounds playful, he may simply be singing, perhaps because he heard a siren. In the wild, wolves have howling sessions—they're social events.

What to say and do:

1. If your dog is merely singing, by all means join in and sing along, or play a harmonica or some other instrument. Your dog won't care if you play badly.

2. If your dog is disturbing you or your neighbors by howling plaintively, startle him with a strong verbal correction in mid-howl. If necessary, use the spray bottle or shaker can. If he remains quiet for a few minutes, stroke and praise him calmly. Spend some time with him and then leave, cautioning him to be quiet. Wait in ambush and repeat the correction if he howls again.

3. Don't try to correct a puppy this way. If your newly arrived pup is howling, set up a pen for him and sleep in the pen with him for the first few nights, or put his pen next to your bed and let your arm dangle into the pen to calm him. Keep him near you at night for a week or so, if necessary, until he stops howling. Keep a radio on softly and give him an old shirt or some other garment that smells like you, and be sure he has a warm, cozy bed. A crate works well.

Why this works: If your dog finds out that howling plaintively gets him no sympathy, he'll stop.

Howling playfully isn't necessarily something you need to stop—unless it disturbs the neighbors. It's a good release for your dog, and if you join him, it becomes a valid bonding exercise.

Prevention: Make sure your dog spends plenty of quality time with you. Let him sleep indoors at night, preferably next to your bed. Practice his obedience training daily, making it upbeat and fun. Spend twenty minutes a day giving him a calming massage, and give him plenty of exercise. Make sure he has lots of toys and things to gnaw on. In his yard, give him a sandbox and a wading pool. If he's indoors a lot, leave the radio on to keep him company. Make sure your dog is not wasting away alone in the yard day after lonely, boring day.

See also:

Afraid to be alone

HUMPING

Problem: My young male dog humps pillows, people's legs, the neighbor's dogs, and whatever else he sees.

Why your dog is doing this: Your young dog is quite simply a victim of his raging hormones.

What to say and do:

1. Whenever your dog begins to hump something, get him in a scruff grip and firmly pry him off, speaking sternly to him. You can also use the shaker can or spray bottle. Order him to sit and calm him with a neck massage.

2. If necessary, keep a leash on him when he is inside with you. Make certain he is wearing a regular collar, not a choke chain, and grab the leash and correct him with a firm snap—easier, sometimes, than a scruff grip.

3. Male dogs sometimes try to hump toddlers who are their size. This can be dangerous if the youngster is knocked down. The instant your dog starts to place his legs on someone, correct him *quickly* and *firmly*. Be consistent with your commands.

4. Humping in pups is often an early sign of dominant and aggressive behavior. These animals are prime candidates for puppy kindergarten training classes, particularly those emphasizing early handling, restraint, and dominance exercises.

Why this works: Consistent and quick correction will show your pup that this behavior, even though it's natural, won't be tolerated.

Prevention: Remove anything your dog is in the habit of humping. Make sure he gets plenty of exercise, since a tired pup usually doesn't have the energy to engage in this type of behavior. Talk with your veterinarian about getting your dog neutered.

Practice some obedience commands with him. Whenever he is about to hump something, have him sit and stay. Praise him for responding, and keep him busy following commands until the urge passes.

HYPERACTIVITY

Problem: My dog never sits still. He's always on the move, unless he's asleep.

Why your dog is doing this: It is not natural for your dog to be constantly agitated. He may not be getting enough exercise, he may be allergic to something in his food or environment, or he may have an imbalance in his system. He may also be reacting to the excessive energy of the people around him.

What to say and do:

1. Give your dog more exercise, preferably off-leash romps in fenced areas. If this is impossible, take him for romps in the park on a 30-foot line, or find a jogger who will run him for you, unless your dog is likely to drag or trip the jogger.

Also play with your dog at home. Retrieving, chase games, hide-and-seek, or just getting goofy will help him let off steam. Make his yard fun and entertaining, with a sandbox, a wading pool, and plenty of toys. Find him a doggy friend to play with on a regular basis. This will give him a good workout as well as canine companionship.

2. Obedience training will also help settle your dog down. He'll learn to focus and to be calm. Practice the obedience commands daily, keeping the training fun and upbeat, but still making him pay attention to you. Work especially on the down-stay, building up to twenty and then thirty minutes.

3. Spend a quiet half hour a day with your dog. Hold your calming massage sessions after he's had some exercise and is less wired. If necessary, utilize the sit-stay command with your dog on-leash to get him to be still so you can massage him.

4. Check your dog's diet thoroughly and read all the labels on everything you are feeding him, including treats. Put him on a natural-foods diet that is free from food coloring, sweeteners, preservatives, and artificial additives. If he's on a one-meal-a-day diet, feed him two.

5. Examine his environment. Is he allergic to your rug shampoo, kennel disinfectant, gasoline fumes in the garage, or flea killers? Talk to a naturopathic holistic veterinarian, who may be able to give him harmless natural remedies to balance his system.

6. Make sure your dog spends plenty of time in the house with you. Dogs who are abandoned outside become so desperate for attention and companionship that when they do come inside, they're frantic. Keep him inside at least long enough to settle down—and then some.

Let him sleep in your room at night, especially if you are away from him all day. This time spent near you at night, listening to you breathe and toss around, will be soothing to him because he is near you, his pack family. Even if he must sleep in a crate in your room, the time there will still be nourishing and calming.

Why this works: Exercise will release his nervous energy, and obedience training helps him to learn self-control, gives him a way to please you, and counts as quality time.

The massage helps to calm him down and gives you both a chance to spend some mellow time together. The house time lets him be with his pack, which makes him feel more secure.

A toxin-free diet and environment gives his body a chance to become as healthy and balanced as possible.

Prevention: Start your dog on an obedience training program right away. Make sure he is not pining away in the yard, isolated from you, and give him plenty of exercise.

Make sure his diet is healthy and that he is free of parasites, internal and external.

If your household is very busy or noisy, give your dog a quiet place to retreat to where he can rest undisturbed.

Check your own emotional state and see if you could be contributing to his fast-paced life. If so, take steps to calm yourself (yoga is a great help).

See also:
Excitable behavior
Wild behavior in the house
Zooming

IGNORING YOU

Problem: My dog just ignores me when I yell at him. He pays no attention to my commands.

Why your dog is doing this: Some dogs are more willful than others. Certain breeds, such as terriers, were bred to be tenacious in their pursuit of varmints. Northern breeds, such as malamutes and huskies, were bred to pull sleds, not to cater to the whims of humans. Hounds were bred to follow game. Your dog, like his ancestors, is not all that interested in pleasing you, and if you are always yelling, he'll just tune you out.

What to say and do:

1. Establish your position as leader of the pack by putting your dog through a thorough basic obedience program. Make this activity fun for your dog; praise him a lot and feed his ego, making it pleasant for him to cooperate with you. Mix training, play, and massage.

2. Spend twenty minutes each day giving him a calming massage to his neck area. Relax him until he drops his head. Don't pet him or give him affection without first asking him to follow a simple obedience command, and keep the petting to a minimum. Make him work for praise and attention until he understands that he must earn your affection and that he doesn't get praised just for existing.

3. Be gentle with him in your daily interactions. Keep your voice down and speak respectfully to him. Make sure there is a huge contrast between your normal voice and your correctional voice, so he can hear the difference.

Why this works: If you use the obedience training to elevate you to pack leader, your dog will be much more interested in pleasing you. If the amount of free (unearned) affection he gets is kept to a minimum, he will become more eager to do whatever it takes to get his much-needed dose of love.

Prevention: If you endlessly nag at your dog, or if you shout all the time, your dog will simply tune you out. Speak to your dog in a normal voice.

Feed your dog one or two meals a day to help him see you as the pack leader who provides him with food. Have him sit and stay before you put his bowl down or give him a treat, so that he knows he must do something to please you before he gets his food.

Make sure he gets plenty of exercise and has a daily routine that is interesting and meets his need for companionship, house time, quiet time, training, play, and exercise.

If he is an intact male, have him neutered.

JUMPING INTO THE POOL

Problem: My dog jumped into a swimming pool and couldn't get out. We had to rescue her. I'm afraid she'll do this again and drown.

Why your dog is doing this: Some dogs aren't aware of what a pool of water is until they jump into one and panic. Other dogs love to swim but don't understand swimming pools with steep, slippery sides and underwater steps.

What to say and do:

1. Teach your dog how to get out of the pool. Go in and out of the water with her many times until she learns how to use the steps. Swim around the pool with her and take her back to the stairs, saying, "Let's go find the steps."

2. If she likes to jump off the edge, call her over to the stairs as soon as she hits the water, or if she is retrieving something, wait until she has the object in her mouth and then call her to the stairs.

3. Even if your dog isn't interested in the water, you should teach her how to swim and how to get out of the pool. Get in the pool and coax her in slowly, patting your leg and taking your time. Have a toy to entice her and talk to her happily. If necessary, guide her gently down the last few steps into the water so she is swimming. Let her turn around immediately and swim back to the stairs, if that's what she wants to do. Repeat this procedure daily, encouraging her to swim farther and guiding her back to the steps.

Why this works: Being a guide for your dog and swimming with her to and from the stairs gives her a chance to learn how to exit the pool when she isn't panicked, disoriented, or overexcited.

Prevention: When you are in the water with your dog, be careful that she does not try to climb on top of you, as some dogs will do, especially if they are novice swimmers.

If you don't want your dog in the pool at all, put an area fence around the pool; this will work for kids too. Pool covers are useful only if they are strong enough to hold your dog's weight if she happens to jump on one. If the cover sinks under your dog's weight, it can trap and drown her.

Also, use good common sense: rinse all the chlorine off your dog after her swim or it will irritate her skin.

JUMPING ON FURNITURE

Problem: My dog loves the couch. He has his favorite spot where he likes to settle in.

Why your dog is doing this: Dogs are creatures of comfort who naturally seek out cozy places to rest. In the wild they often lie with their backs against something for support and protection. They also like to perch on an elevated place that gives them a vast horizon. Also, as dogs age, they need softer beds with good back support. Your couch offers many of those features.

What to say and do:

1. Provide your dog with a cozy bed and put it in a room he prefers. If you have a large house, place beds in several areas. If you find your dog on the furniture, tell him, "Get off." If necessary, pull him off gently. Then lead him to his own cozy bed and say, "This is your bed." Don't be rough; be a patient teacher.

2. If he continues to jump on the furniture, pull him off and reprimand him firmly: "You stay off of my couch!" Take him to his bed and put him in a down-stay, praising him if he obeys. If that doesn't work, use the shaker can.

3. If you are on the couch when he tries to jump up, push him off firmly, following the sequence above. If necessary, keep a shaker can hidden behind a cushion.

4. When you find him voluntarily resting in his own bed, praise him warmly: "What a good boy," and stroke him calmly.

Why this works: Giving your dog a comfortable bed of his own answers his basic need for a secure, cozy den. Consistently correcting him for getting on the furniture and then guiding him to his own equally comfortable bed gives him a clear message, and a clear alternative.

Prevention: Provide your dog with a cozy bed that has a soft backrest; the more comfy the bed, the less appealing your furniture will look.

Let your dog know the rules the moment he enters the house, and stick to them. If you allow him on the couch when you're home, don't expect him to stay off the couch when you're out. If you see your dog eyeballing the couch, tell him "No! You stay off the couch!" Direct him to his bed and praise him. If you want to cuddle your dog, put a special mat on the floor for both of you or designate one piece of furniture that he is allowed on.

If you decide to let him on the furniture it is important that he get off when you tell him to. If you encounter any dominance problems such as growling, snapping, or biting, don't let him on the furniture at all. Give him his own bed on the floor.

The only way to guarantee that your dog stays off your furniture is to keep him out of the room when you can't be there to supervise him. If that is impossible, prop a baby gate up across the front of the couch or lay it down on the cushions of the couch to deter him from jumping up on it.

Big shorthaired breeds such as Great Danes, Doberman pinschers, and greyhounds need a soft supportive bed. If they have a warm, cozy, draft-free bed, they will become less arthritic as they grow older. All of these breeds are known to be couch potatoes and enjoy soft bedding; some love to have a blanket thrown over them when it's cold. The smaller shorthaired breeds such as whippets and dachshunds also love comfort and warmth and need cozy beds.

See also:
Crate training

JUMPING ON ME

Problem: When my dog greets me or gets excited or wants attention he jumps on me.

Why your dog is doing this: When your dog greets you, he wants to say hello to your face and hands, not your feet. The best way he knows to get your attention is to get in your face.

What to say and do:

1. As your dog jumps on you, say firmly, "Stay off!" and abruptly yank him downward by the collar, the leash, or the scruff grip. Barring this, surprise him with the shaker can or spray bottle the instant he jumps, or bump him lightly on the nose with your open palm—how foolish of him not to have noticed your hand!

2. Calmly and quietly grasp his paws and casually hold on to them until he gets uncomfortable and starts to squirm. Then gently let him down.

3. Once all four feet are back on the ground, bend down to his level and pet him slowly. Give him the touch he needs while he wiggles around. If he is very bouncy, hold on to his collar to keep him from climbing on you.

4. Before you rise, caution him to "Stay off!" and give him a reminder tug downward on the collar while giving him the stay signal with your other hand. Stand up slowly. If he starts to jump, repeat the correction.

Why this works: If he consistently finds jumping on you to be unpleasant, and if he learns that he gets greeted and touched when he is on the ground, he'll think twice about jumping. Petting him with slow hands helps calm him down.

Prevention: Anticipate when he will jump and warn him not to while he is still thinking about it. If he knows how to sit, have him do so before you pet him. Or have him sit after you've corrected him. You are telling him it's bad to jump, good to sit, and good to be calm and get petted.

Obedience training will teach him to control his body and take your corrections seriously. A minimum of twenty minutes a day of calming massage will help him to see how pleasant it is to be still and get touched.

Don't absentmindedly pet your dog when he jumps on you. Be consistent with your corrections. Ignoring the jumping won't work, either. With young puppies, bend down as quickly as possible so they never get in the habit of jumping up.

Keep a shaker can or spray bottle by your front door. Keep a leash on your dog when you're with him if that makes it easier for you to control him.

JUMPING ON OTHER ADULTS

Problem: My dog loves everyone and jumps up on people wildly when he says hello.

Why your dog is doing this: Your dog does not want to greet people's feet; he wants to greet faces and hands, so he jumps up to reach those parts and get noticed.

What to say and do:

1. You must make sure your dog understands that he cannot jump on you before you can expect him to take you seriously and control himself around others.

2. Have your dog on a leash when you approach a new person and command him to sit and stay. If he ignores the command and starts to jump, correct him by snapping the leash quickly and saying, "Off, stay off!" If he leaps several times in a row, pop him back off each time with a firm leash snap and a stern command until he finally stops jumping and listens to you. Then make him sit and stay and praise him: "Good sit." Calm him with a massage.

3. Keep him seated and under control with your right hand while you massage him with your left hand. When he is calm and under control let the other adult pet him, and ask that person to bend down to the dog's level and pet him slowly so as not to excite him.

4. Watch your dog closely, and if he even begins to think about jumping, give him a reminder tug downward and warn him to "Stay off." Alternate between the correction-control and the praise-massage as needed.

5. If your dog does not respond to the leash correction, use the shaker can or spray bottle along with the leash snap. Keep a shaker can or spray bottle near the front door, and take the spray bottle on walks.

6. If your dog is off-leash and jumps on someone, use the shaker can or spray bottle, or grab him by the collar or scruff and pull him off abruptly, telling him, "Off, stay off!"

Why this works: Correcting your dog every time he tries to jump on someone lets him know you will not tolerate it. This sequence tells your dog that it is bad to jump, good to sit, and good to calm down, which you help him do. He learns that he won't get petted until he's controlled himself.

Prevention: Obedience training to teach control, and daily twenty-minute sessions of calming massage, will teach your dog to maintain a sit position and calm down. This self-control will transfer easily to greetings and jumping up. If necessary, keep a leash on him in the house, for easy grabbing. If he even thinks of jumping, warn him, "Hey! Stay off!" Don't roughhouse with your dog and let him jump on you, and don't let others do so either. Ask other people to get down to his level to say hello. If he is a small dog, give him a pedestal to jump onto in your house so he can be higher up for easy greetings.

JUMPING OUT OF THE CAR WINDOW

Problem: My dog has jumped out of the car window several times. I'm terrified he'll be killed.

Why you dog is doing this: He doesn't have a clue as to how dangerous his actions could be if the car is moving or in traffic. What's more, he has no car manners. This is fun for him.

What to say and do:

1. Set your dog up for an ambush. Park your car in a quiet place, away from traffic, such as your driveway or an alley. Leave him in the car with the window wide open and stand a few feet away, totally ignoring him. Talk to a friend, and ask another friend to walk his dog along the sidewalk.

2. When your dog puts his feet on the door and starts to hoist himself out the window, rush him and grab him by the scruff or whatever you can get hold of. Shove him abruptly and unmercifully back inside the car, scolding very harshly.

3. Lecture him firmly for ten to fifteen seconds as you pin him to the seat: "You stay in the car!" Turn away and ignore him, offering no kind words. Repeat this procedure until you get the message across clearly.

4. If he seems unfazed by the correction, add the shaker can or spray bottle. If that doesn't work, ask a obedience trainer to help you teach car manners.

5. If your dog tries to jump out of the car while you are inside with him, put a leash on him and sit in the car, casually ignoring him. When he tries to jump out, yank him sharply and tell him to stay in the car. Have a helper wait outside of the car and use the spray bottle or shaker can on your dog at the same time.

Why this works: Setting your dog up for an ambush allows you to correct him before he is out the window. Because this behavior could be life-threatening to your dog, yourself, or other drivers, you must impress upon your dog the seriousness of the offense. By using a very severe voice tone and very startling and scary hand movements or leash snaps (saved only for situations such as these), you will make a lasting impression on your dog.

Prevention: Start obedience training early and teach car manners (entering and exiting on command only), so your dog will associate the car with self-control. Keep your windows closed so as to prevent escapes until your dog is more reliable. Be careful of electric window buttons that your dog could activate with his paws. Crating him when he's in the car until he learns to behave works well too.

See also:
Bolting from the car

JUMPING OVER FENCES

Problem: My dog keeps jumping over the fence and getting out of the yard. I'm afraid he's going to get killed on the road or lost.

Why your dog is doing this: Your dog is bored and wants to explore the exciting world beyond the fence.

What to say and do:

1. If you can catch your dog in the act, startle him with the scruff grip, shaker can, spray bottle, or garden hose. Sound very angry and give him a serious lecture.

2. If he has found places where he can climb the fence, remove his footholds and make the fence unscalable.

3. If all other techniques fail, install an electric fence wire designed for small animals. Run a strand of hot wire at the height his paws will hit when he jumps on the fence. He will touch it once and probably never approach the fence again. Flag the wire with survey tape and leave it on for a couple of weeks. After a while you can usually turn the fence off.

Why this works: The electric fence wire is a sure bet for controlling fence jumping, but you must also provide a good life for your dog that includes house time, exercise, and a fun yard. Otherwise he will be miserable and lonely.

Prevention: Make sure your dog is not living his entire life in the yard. A bored, neglected dog will want to leave his home. Never let your dog put his feet on, or jump up on, a fence, exercise pen, or baby gate. When he is young, teach him to accept being behind a baby gate in the house so he will learn to respect barriers early on. Confine him in an adequately fenced yard from the start. If you have a low fence and you slowly raise it, you are teaching your dog to jump higher and higher.

Make your dog's yard entertaining by providing him with fun things to do. A sandbox, a wading pool, toys, and things to gnaw on, a cozy doghouse, adequate shade, and fresh water all make a dog's area fun.

Let your dog spend time with you in the house; this will help him feel he has a home he doesn't want to leave. Let him sleep inside at night, preferably in your room; it is soothing and bonding for your dog to sleep near you.

Daily exercise is essential for keeping your dog happy. Long walks, romps in the park, another dog to play with, and car rides to fun places with interesting smells will all help make your dog happier and less bored. A tired dog is less likely to go exploring.

Obedience training will teach your dog to take you seriously, so when you do correct him for jumping the fence, he might take it to heart. Practice the obedience commands in the yard. If he gets interested in things on the other side of the fence, get his attention back on the commands, and give him lots of praise for cooperating.

See also:
  Roaming
  Running away

LEASH, FEAR OF

Problem: My young dog is afraid to walk on-leash. If I try to pull her, she won't budge.

Why your dog is doing this: Your dog is frightened of the pressure on her neck. She is sure the leash is going to strangle her, because it literally has her by the throat.

What to say and do:

1. Use a buckle collar on your dog, rather than a choke chain.

2. On walking lessons carry treats your dog loves, such as bologna, cooked liver, cheese, or tuna. Put the food in your right hand, hiding most of it in your fist. In your left hand, hold the leash.

3. Give your dog a taste of the food and try to get her to follow you—hold the treat right in front of her nose if necessary. If she follows, feed her as she walks with you. Keep the leash slack so there is no pressure on her neck. Speak happily and be very encouraging.

4. If she doesn't follow, or if she stops walking, slide your left hand one foot down the leash, squat down, and put light, steady forward tension on the leash. *Don't jerk her.* Entice her by holding the food a few inches from her nose while you keep the tension on the leash. If she takes a step forward (the leash will go slack), let her have the treat, praise her lavishly, and encourage her to follow you. Repeat this sequence, making her walk a little farther each time to get the treat.

5. If she bucks and rears, as most puppies will do when you put tension on the leash, back away from her a few feet to give her room to struggle. Remain squatting and continue to hold on to the leash. Again, *don't jerk her.* She will soon stop struggling and discover she's still alive. Now resume the food-lure method.

6. Once she starts to follow you more readily on a loose leash, make occasional contact with little tugs on her neck, so she'll experience the collar pressure in a nonthreatening way.

7. If she is too frightened to move, get her used to the sensation of collar pressure when she's not wearing a leash by gently teaching her to sit and then to stand back up again. To get her to stand up, pull her collar ever so gently forward from under her throat while you lift her up under her belly and say, "Stand." Scratch her belly and neck, praise her, feed her a treat, and then guide her into the sit while saying, "Sit," and using her collar or your hand on her throat to mimic the tug of the collar. Practice this sequence until she is used to the pressure on her neck as a signal. Then you can get her used to walking on-leash.

Why this works: When you put a slight forward tension on the leash and lure your dog with food, she will move toward you, the leash will slacken, and she will learn that moving forward relieves the pressure on her neck.

Prevention: Get your dog used to a collar before attempting any leash lessons. When she's accustomed to the collar, let her drag a short, light leash around. Her leash shouldn't have a huge snap on it that bangs into her. Match the equipment to the size of the dog.

Never put a choke chain on a dog as a first collar. The tightening sensation might terrify her. Don't jerk or drag your dog, as this will also scare her. You want her first associations with the leash to be positive.

LEASH, PULLING ON

Problem: My dog drags me down the street like a sled. I've tried to teach her to heel, but she won't slow down!

Why your dog is doing this: Your dog just wants to move faster; walking is boring and not much of a workout. When you hold her back on a tight leash with steady pressure, it's natural for her to resist and create tension.

What to say and do:

1. Attach a 6-foot leash to your dog's collar, and work with her in your home, holding her loosely on the leash and watching her closely. When she starts to walk away, give her a leash snap before she tightens the leash and tell her firmly, "No! No pulling, stay close!" Snap her just a little harder than she would have pulled you. Then pat your leg and invite her over for a scratch, saying, "Good girl." Repeat until she learns to wait for you on a slack leash.

2. Take her for a walk around your house. Tell her, "Rosie, stay close," slap your leg, and walk off. If she moves too far from you, quickly pivot around before she tightens the leash and move away in the opposite direction. Pat your leg as you walk, and encourage her to catch up with you.

3. Practice in the yard, pivoting and using the leash snap each time she's about to pull on you. As she improves, work your way out to the sidewalk and beyond.

Why this works: By suddenly changing directions every time she forges ahead, you teach her to watch you closely, control herself, and stay with you.

Prevention: Before you take your dog for a walk, spend twenty minutes playing with her in the house, the yard, or the park. Allow her to let off some steam, then take her for her walk.

If your dog's only exercise is her on-leash walk, she will have difficulty controlling herself. Consider walking her on a spring-loaded leash so that she can stretch her legs. Signal her with the leash snap before she starts pulling you around. She may not pull as hard on the longer leash because she'll have time to stop and sniff and then catch up. Make sure your dog is getting enough exercise in the yard and in parks—off-leash, if it's safe. If you can't let her off-leash, get a 30- to 50-foot cord and let her romp around on that. She will be much happier.

Spend twenty minutes a day giving her a calming massage, working especially on her neck. Since she's been pulling on you a lot, her neck tissue may be tough, thickened, and insensitive.

LICKING PEOPLE

Problem: My dog just loves people and slobbers kisses on everyone she meets.

Why your dog is doing this: Licking is a sign of submission and affection. Your dog expresses her pleasure by licking people.

What to say and do:

1. Don't worry too much about this. If people don't want to be kissed by your dog they don't have to visit with her!

2. If you want to control the licking, keep the greetings low-key, and don't let her get too excited. Teach her to sit and stay so she will be able to calm herself before she gets petted.

3. Spend twenty minutes a day giving her a calming massage. This will teach her to receive affection without having to return it.

4. Teach her what "kissing" means. When she licks your hands, tell her, "Give me a kiss—good girl." After a few licks, say, "That's enough kissing, thank you," and distract her with the sit-stay command and some slow massage.

5. Have your dog sit and stay and calm her with some slow stroking before she greets people. Ask your friends to open their hands so your dog can give them a hello kiss while you tell her, "Say hello—give him a kiss." Then tell her, "That's enough kissing," and gently restrain her with calm stroking hands. Don't correct her for licking; just calm her.

Why this works: Putting a word ("kissing") to the action of licking makes your dog aware of what she is doing and that you are a part of it. The daily massage session combined with the sit-stay will help her calm down and control her tongue.

Prevention: Licking is a natural behavior for dogs and should not be entirely discouraged. If people are worried about germs, tell them that a dog's tongue is fairly antiseptic. Be happy you have a friendly dog who wants to shower people with love—she could be snapping or growling instead. It is not something you want to prevent, just monitor.

LICKING, SCRATCHING, AND CHEWING HERSELF

Problem: My dog keeps licking, scratching, and chewing on herself—sometimes to the point where she creates sores on her body.

Why your dog is doing this: Excessive self-grooming can be either physical or emotional in origin, and sometimes both. Her behavior may indicate a reaction to diet, household toxins, cleansers, shampoos, flea killers, or insect bites. If she doesn't seem to be allergic to any of these substances, her behavior could indicate boredom, stress, or neglect.

What to say and do:

1. Read the labels on everything you feed your dog, including treats, to make sure that her diet is as natural and chemical-free as possible. Eliminate all foods with sweeteners and all artificial flavorings, colorings, and preservatives. Specialty pet food stores carry a wide variety of dog foods that are free of toxic ingredients. Many books about dog health include simple, nutritious recipes for natural foods your dog will love.

2. Have your dog checked by your veterinarian for skin parasites such as fleas, lice, ticks, or mange mites. If any are present, use the least toxic shampoo available for ridding her of these pests. At the same time, treat your house, yard, car, doghouse, crate, and dog bedding, also with the least toxic product available. Your local health food store probably carries a variety of organic flea-control products, or your veterinarian can supply you with the appropriate medication.

3. Make sure you are not using dog shampoos, rug shampoos, or yard sprays that leave an irritating toxic residue.

4. If your dog feels bored and neglected, she may be relieving her boredom and giving herself attention by grooming herself and scratching. You need to establish a routine that will brighten up her life. Daily obedience training, play sessions, romps in the park, rides in the car, and doggy playmates will go a long way toward improving the quality of her life.

5. If the only time you acknowledge your dog is to yell at her for licking, she may lick to get you to notice her; to her, negative attention is better than none. Obedience training, massage, and playtime will give your dog the quality attention she needs.

6. Give your dog interesting things to gnaw on, such as cow hooves or beef marrow bones. When the marrow is gone, smear some cheese or liverwurst inside the bone. This will give her something to lick instead of herself.

7. Apply Bitter Apple or aloe vera to hot spots to deter licking. Hot spots are the inflamed, raw areas where you dog has chewed on her skin.

Why this works: Looking at an excessive scratching and chewing problem holistically offers you different angles of approach; you are treating your dog's life and habits as a whole instead of applying a Band-Aid solution. If you simply have a vet give your dog a cortisone shot to stop the licking, you will do nothing to eliminate the cause, and the dog will return to licking herself.

Prevention: A natural diet, plenty of love, fresh air, exercise, a clean, well-groomed body, and a healthy environment, combined with plenty of companionship and training, will create a healthy, content dog who will be less likely to lick from nerves or ill health.

MEDICINE

Problem: My dog squirms away from me when I apply external medicine, especially if he has a rash or an ear infection.

Why your dog is doing this: Your dog knows what's coming—something unpleasant—so he starts to struggle as soon as you try to hold him still.

What to say and do:

1. Spend at least twenty minutes a day doing calming massage with your dog when you have no intention of applying the medication. This way, he will relax and accept being held still, and he'll learn being held precedes a nice massage. Work your way slowly to the trouble area, and gently massage the area near the sore spot. He may wiggle, anticipating pain, and then find that the massage actually feels good. If your touch does cause any pain, lighten up and work on adjacent areas. Remember, the key here is to give your dog a good experience so that he will look forward to being held still.

2. When you need to administer the medication, settle your dog down with a calming massage. If necessary, have a helper distract him with food as you quickly apply the medication. Then offer him his favorite treat.

Why this works: By holding your dog still during soothing, pleasant massage sessions, you will show him that being held still for his medicine is a very brief unpleasant break in an otherwise enjoyable experience.

Prevention: If you practice early handling exercises on your dog while he is still a puppy, he will learn to accept being held, and will think of this experience as a pleasant one. The trust that develops in those early sessions will help your dog realize that when you do something unpleasant to him, it is because it really must be done, not because you want to hurt him in any way.

MOUTHING. SEE NIPPING AND MOUTHING PEOPLE'S HANDS

NAIL CUTTING

Problem: My dog hates to have his nails trimmed. He struggles so hard that I'm afraid I'll injure him.

Why your dog is doing this: If the quick inside the nails is cut or squeezed when the nail is trimmed, it can be painful. Your dog may have bad memories of such an experience in the past.

What to say and do:

1. Spend twenty minutes a day giving your dog a calming massage. A small dog can sit on the couch with you or on a countertop covered with a comfortable blanket. A large dog can sit on the floor, with you behind him on a couch. If your dog ends up lying down, that's great! The idea is to get him relaxed.

2. When your dog responds to the massage by relaxing, slowly work your way down one of his legs, gently massaging the skin and hair. If he starts to flinch, retreat a bit and continue massaging the area he will allow you to work. As he relaxes, continue on down his leg. Eventually you will be able to massage his feet—be patient. Once he allows you to rub his feet, click your ring or a thimble lightly against the nail until he stops flinching. It may take several massage sessions to reach this point.

3. When you are ready to clip his nails, set up in the same location. Relax him as usual with the massage and click his nails with the clippers this time. Then slowly and carefully clip only the very tip off one nail. Use only a sharp, high-quality dog-nail clipper. Talk to your dog in soft, reassuring tones. If you show confidence in what you are doing, he will read this and will have confidence that you will not hurt him. Praise him continually for holding still. Clip a few more nails. Go slowly and carefully.

4. If you can, enlist a helper to scratch on his favorite body spots so he is distracted by a good sensation. If he is still worried about the clippers, have your helper feed him some treats while you carefully continue clipping.

Why this works: The massage sessions show your dog that he can trust your hands, and that you are sensitive to him and his body. Once he believes in you and feels safe, he will let you cut his nails.

Prevention: Never let anyone deliberately cut your dogs nails into the quick. If your dog has light-colored nails, you can see the quick. Be sure to cut a bit closer to the tip of the nail. With black-nailed dogs, cut just a bit at a time, shaving off slivers. You can then file you dog's nails to the desired length. If you are still uncertain, watch a professional to see how it is done.

The more positive, hands-on calming and massage exercises you practice with your dog at an early age, the fewer problems you'll experience in cutting his nails later.

NERVOUSNESS

Problem: My dog always seems nervous about one thing or another. He paces around worriedly with his tail tucked between his legs.

Why your dog is doing this: Your dog is fearful and is constantly on the alert for things that might scare or hurt him.

What to say and do:

1. Basic obedience training is essential for helping nervous dogs calm down and focus. After your dog has learned a few commands, you can distract him from things that scare him by asking him to focus on the training commands.

2. Spend a minimum of twenty minutes a day giving your dog a calming massage in a quiet, distraction-free place. It is important for you to be relaxed too. Once your dog has learned to relax under your hands, use the calming massage any time he's upset. He must sit first, control his body, and listen to you before you begin the massage.

3. Examine his diet closely. Any artificial ingredients, sugar or sugar substitutes, colorings, or preservatives could be adversely affecting your dog's nervous system. Feed him a natural diet, including treats. Have your dog examined by a veterinarian, preferably a holistic vet who may be able to calm your dog's nerves with natural remedies and help your dog's body return to a balanced state.

4. If there are specific things that scare your dog, practice the obedience work with those things at a safe distance at first, and bring them closer as he relaxes. Incorporate the massage into the training sessions.

5. When your dog is frightened, try to distract him with a game or a treat. This will help take his mind off whatever is worrying him and switch his focus to you.

Why this works: Obedience training will give your dog confidence and teach him to control himself, even when he's nervous. The massage will help release the tension in his body.

Prevention: Make sure that your own actions are not scaring your dog. When you correct your dog, keep your voice and hands as mild as possible. Nervous dogs are usually very sensitive. By over-correcting him, you will contribute to his nervousness.

If there is a lot of yelling in your house, try to tone it down. If necessary turn to your dog and reassure him in a gentle tone that he's okay and that you're not mad at him.

Don't let anyone tease your dog or intentionally startle him. If you have children, make sure they are not pestering him. Give your dog a bed or crate that he can retreat to, and make sure he gets plenty of exercise so that he'll tire himself out and use up any excess energy that might be channeled into nervousness.

See also:
> Abused dog
> Fear of certain objects
> Hand-shyness
> Shyness

New Dog, Introducing

Problem: We're getting another dog and we aren't sure how to introduce our current dog to the new one.

What to say and do:

1. If you acquire a full-grown dog, let the two dogs meet on neutral territory—in a park or a field—not at your home or in any other place that is uniquely your veteran dog's territory. If the dogs are good off-leash, two people can bring the dogs to the park from opposite ends and let them meet alone, away from the distractions of people. If you can't let them off-leash, take them for a walk together. Keep the leashes loose, talk happily, and don't let the leashes get tangled.

2. If you're bringing home a puppy, you'll still want to let the dogs meet on neutral ground, if possible, or in the front yard. Talk very happily to your grown dog about this new puppy you've brought home.

3. Leave the dogs alone together only when you are sure they get along. Don't worry if your dog snaps at the pup for climbing all over him; that's your dog's way of telling the pup to respect him. But if your puppy is driving your older dog crazy, make sure your older dog has a place to escape to. Crating one or the other for short periods, sectioning off rooms with baby gates, or putting a puppy run in your backyard will help.

4. Make sure you give your original dog the same amount of attention and exercise that he always got, including one-on-one time with you. If possible, give him more attention than ever. Provide the new dog with her own bed, food bowl, water dish, and toys.

5. Practice obedience work with both dogs together so they see that you are their pack leader and they need to listen to you, alone or together. Give them calming massages side by side (that's why we have two hands!).

Why this works: It's easier for dogs to form friendships if they meet on neutral ground. Dogs are pack animals and like the company of other dogs, but asking them to meet for the first time in your house or yard will make the newcomer seem like an intruder.

Prevention: Avoid having the dogs meet in your home or yard, so that no territorial issue will develop. Also, dogs of the opposite sex usually get along better than same-sex dogs, though if males are neutered young enough, they are usually compatible. Pick a breed that is not known to be dominant and bossy. Dogs of the same breed usually enjoy each other's company and have similar playing styles.

NIPPING AND MOUTHING PEOPLE'S HANDS

Problem: Whenever we pet our dog, she puts her mouth all over our hands. She's not trying to bite us, but sometimes she nips at our hands.

Why your dog is doing this: Your dog sees your hands as delightful toys. When you grab at her, your hands seem like the mouth of another dog, and since she doesn't respect you as her pack leader, she won't stop nibbling and nipping when you tell her to stop.

What to say and do:

1. Keep your dog on a leash when you're home. (Use a leash without a loop handle so it won't get caught on things.) As soon as she moves into attack mode, give her a couple of quick leash snaps and tell her, "Leave it, no bite!" Put her in a sit and calm her down with a slow massage.

2. The instant she grabs at your hands when she's off-leash, use your free hand to do the scruff grip, telling her sharply, "Leave it, no bite!" Don't yank your hand out of her mouth; let her spit it out. *Relax the scruff grip slowly and ease into a soothing massage.* Be prepared to repeat the scruff grip if she starts to mouth or nip you again. Correct her just as she begins to open her mouth—if possible before she gets ahold of you.

3. If this doesn't work, cram your hand *sideways* into the dog's mouth until the side of your hand is wedged up against the corners of her mouth. Hold it there for a few seconds. Then let her go and calm her with a massage.

4. Use the spray bottle or shaker can, if necessary, as soon as she makes her move. If she persists, squirt some lemon juice into her mouth from one of those lemon-shaped yellow plastic containers sold in supermarkets.

Why this works: Correcting your dog every time she tries to mouth you lets her know you won't tolerate mouthing and nipping at all. By consistently demonstrating your displeasure, you're showing her that this is not a game. The calming massage lets her experience your hands as controlling and soothing rather than as toys to chew on.

Prevention: Teach your dog some basic obedience commands so she'll learn to respect you and take you seriously. Correct her if she nips at you; then calm her and resume the obedience lesson.

Move your hands very slowly around your dog's head. Don't rough-house with her, play tug-of-war, or bonk her head playfully. Never put your fingers in your dog's mouth, and show your family and friends how to use their hands on her.

Spend twenty minutes a day giving your dog a calming massage with slow hands.

Give her toys to play with and gnaw on. This will keep her mouth busy. Let her chew toys while you pet and cuddle with her.

NIPPING AT CLOTHES AND ANKLES

Problem: My dog nips at my feet and ankles and tugs at my clothing with her mouth. She does this to my kids too, and it's hard to shake her off.

Why your dog is doing this: To your dog, any moving target is something to chase, just the way her ancestors chased other animals in the wild. When you try to shake her off, your action becomes part of the game.

What to say and do:

1. Use the shaker can or spray bottle to surprise her the instant she begins to go after you. Tell her very firmly, "No, leave it!" Praise her when she stops and direct her to a more suitable toy.

2. If your dog is small, as soon as she dives for your legs, startle her by quickly pushing her to the ground with both hands spread over her shoulder area. Don't hurt her; hold her gently but firmly. Do the scruff grip, if necessary, along with the shoulder hold. Firmly tell her, "No, leave it!" Keep lecturing her and holding her still on the ground until she settles down. Then relax your hold and ease into a calming massage, slowly let her get up, and guide her to an appropriate toy.

3. If your dog is large, do the scruff grip or grab her by the collar. Hold her still while you lecture her firmly. Ease into a calming massage and, after you let her go, direct her to a better toy.

4. If the nipping continues, let your dog drag her leash around when you are with her. This way, you can grab it and give a few quick leash snaps when necessary. Be careful. Don't use a leash with a loop on the end that might get caught on something, and be sure to attach the leash to a regular collar, not a choke chain—or she could choke herself. Use the leash in conjunction with the spray bottle, if necessary.

5. Once you've learned how to correct your dog for going after you, you must teach her not to go after your kids. When your dog makes a grab for one of your children, correct her with whatever works best—the shaker can, leash snap, spray bottle, or scruff grip and pounce—and then direct her to an appropriate toy. If your kids are old enough, let them use the shaker can or spray bottle.

6. Give your dog large, enticing toys to focus on and play with. Try dragging an old bedspread tied in knots or a branch of a tree to keep her farther away from human bodies when she's playing. The temptation for her to nip at your heels should diminish when she sees this interesting object being dragged behind you.

Why this works: Consistent corrections, combined with the control and respect gained through obedience training, will teach your dog to take you seriously. The calming massage together with suitable toys will show your dog how you want her to behave.

Prevention: Teach your dog some basic obedience commands so she will learn to respect you. Spend twenty minutes a day practicing the commands with her, allowing no distractions. When she has learned the commands alone with you, practice around the kids.

Spend twenty minutes a day doing a calming massage to give you and your dog some peaceful time together and to help you calm her quickly when she gets nippy.

Anticipate when your dog is about to dive for someone's feet and warn her with strong words and, if necessary, use the leash snap, spray bottle, or shaker can to stop her before she carries through.

Provide your dog with toys that are more fun to play with than toes and give her plenty of exercise, because a tired dog will not have the energy to chase your feet around all day.

NOISES, FEAR OF

Problem: My dog is so frightened of loud noises—everything from thunder to the television—that she gets upset and hides.

Why your dog is doing this: It is natural for a dog to seek shelter when she hears thunder or other loud, sharp sounds. In the wild, thunderstorms can be dangerous. The shriek of a cougar or the trumpeting of an elephant can signal danger as well. Wild canines sought shelter when they heard such noises, and so your dog hides in her closet-cave for protection. Her fear could also result from a scary experience in her past; she may have been too close to firecrackers or gunshots.

What to say and do:

1. Let her stay in the closet, if she feels safe and protected there. Make a comfortable bed for her, so she knows it's okay to retreat to her safe haven. Turn some music on in the room to help mask the sounds that frighten her.

2. Try to get her used to the noises. Either make or buy a tape recording—tapes of thunderstorms are available. Play the tape at a low volume while you do something fun and distracting with your dog—some upbeat obedience work, for example—and then give her some treats.

3. Increase the volume of the tape as your dog gets used to the noises. Because she is terrified of these loud sounds, you must proceed slowly, giving her time to recondition herself. If you scare her even once, you'll lose all the ground you've gained and you will have to start all over again.

4. If sudden loud noises, such as a cupboard door slamming, scare your dog, have a friend repeat the offending sound over and over again, at lower volumes and at a distance, while you perform the fun distraction work with the dog.

5. Teach your dog what "cookie" means, and whenever she is startled by a noise, quickly get her focused on the cookie: "Suzie, do you want a cookie? Let's go get a cookie!"

6. It would also be a good idea to have her checked out by a holisitic veterinarian who might have a natural remedy to calm your dog during those times that frighten her.

Why this works: Letting your dog retreat to her closet-cave gives her a place to ride out the storm. She is following her instinct to hide in an enclosed dark place, just as she would in the wild.

By practicing commands and playing, you are keeping her busy, and by giving her treats, you are replacing her fear with the immediate gratification of wonderful rewards.

Prevention: Never subject your dog to fireworks, firecrackers, or gunfire. Make sure no one is teasing her through the fence or using a popgun or other noisy toys around her.

If she feels safe in your closet, make a place for her there. Crate-training her and then throwing a cover over the crate during scary times will give her a secure den that she will feel safe in. Don't confine her in the crate unless you are home to watch her—she might panic.

Don't reassure her in a worried tone. If you sound worried, she will think you are scared too. Instead, talk to her in an upbeat voice.

Spend twenty minutes a day giving her a calming massage to relax her. When she is frightened, add some calming massage to the other techniques you use to soothe her.

Make sure your yard and gates are secure. If your dog panics, she might escape and run away in fear.

Give her access to the house during storms, fireworks season, and other times when noise might frighten her—and keep a close watch over her.

See also:
Fearful of objects
Nervousness

OBESITY. SEE OVEREATING

OFF-LEASH MISBEHAVIOR

Problem: My dog does not listen to me when he's off-leash. He won't even come to me when I call him.

Why your dog is doing this: Your dog finds running loose much more fun than staying on-leash with you. He doesn't

come when you call him because he knows it means the end of his
romp.

What to say and do:

1. Review your dog's on-leash obedience training indoors, in your
yard, and then at the park. Every training session should consist of
several three-minute drills, each followed by five minutes of play.
Practice the come command and give him lots of praise when he
comes to you. In the park, keep him on a 30–50-foot cord; this will
give him plenty of room to romp while you still retain some control.
Always take a favorite toy along for him to chase and chew. Remember, "fun" is the key word here. If you make the sessions fun, the
off-leash training period will be a great time for the both of you.

2. Conduct your first off-leash training sessions in a small room
in your house so your dog has less space in which to ignore you.
Warm him up on-leash first, and then take the leash off and do a few
simple, upbeat maneuvers: a couple of quick sit-stays; some heeling
ending with sits; a few sit-stays ending with come; then some play.
Repeat this sequence several times in a row. Do several very short
sessions every day in different small rooms. Always be fun and
engaging, and stay very upbeat. Then move into the larger rooms in
your house, and eventually graduate to your fenced yard.

3. If you have no yard, practice in an enclosed outdoor area such
as a tennis court. If he starts to ignore you, put on his long line and
let him drag it while you hold the end of it. Use it when necessary to
get his attention or back up a command—stepping on the cord works
nicely. Be consistent, and keep the same lesson style—short with
lots of praise. Remember, the key word is "fun."

4. Whenever you are in an unfenced area, use the 50-foot training line, and let your dog drag it while you hold on to the end, making
sure that it doesn't get caught on anything. When he's responding
well to your commands, let go of the drag line. He will simply assume
that you are holding the end of it. As he learns to listen to you, you
can shorten it a couple of feet at a time. He may need to drag a short
line for a long, long time.

5. Carry treats in your pocket whenever you are with your dog,
and periodically call him to you, saying, "Sunny, come! Do you want

a cookie?" Do this at home, in the yard, in the park, and when he is playing with other dogs. When he comes to you, feed him his treat and send him on his way. This will help him realize that coming to you is a good idea, and that when you call him, his fun is not going to end.

Why this works: By keeping your dog's training sessions short and fun, and by following them with playtime, you show him that it's a pleasure to listen to you and hang around with you. By calling your dog when you're at home and before you leave the park, and by giving him a treat and a scratch, you help him see coming to you as something pleasant.

Prevention: Keep your dog off-leash as much as possible as he grows up—always in areas safe from cars, of course—so that being off-leash is no big deal to him. He won't crave freedom so much, because it's always been there.

If you have a dog friend who is obedient off-leash, take him to the park for romps with your dog. In the park, put down a blanket to sit on; have a water bowl for your dogs and a snack for yourself. Establish a base camp that your dog can hang around and return to for a drink, treat, and a loving scratch.

Never call your dog to you for something that he will construe to be unpleasant. When you call him to you at the end of your park romp, make a big fuss over him as you put on his leash and leave so he will continue to associate coming to you with fun.

See also:
Hand-shy
Hard to catch
Roaming
Running away

OLD AGE

Problem: My dog is slowing down as he ages. What special changes should I make for him?

What to say and do:

1. Make sure his diet is appropriate for a less active dog. Don't let him get fat, and feed him natural foods that are free from artificial ingredients.

2. Provide him with a particularly soft, cozy bed, away from drafts and commotion, but do not isolate him. Also, old dogs need back support, so put some cushions around the edge of his bed for him to curl up against.

3. Make sure your floors and stairs are not slippery. If necessary, put down nonskid runners. If he has trouble negotiating the stairs, install a ramp with good footing.

4. If he's used to sleeping on the couch or your bed and can no longer easily jump up or get down, provide him with steps or a ramp—these are commercially available—so he can continue to sleep in his favorite spot. This way he still feels loved and comfortable.

5. See that he still gets exercise. Fresh air and intriguing smells will keep him healthy and entertained. Play fetch if he likes it; just don't throw his stick or toy too far.

6. Take him for regular veterinary checkups and make sure his teeth are kept clean and his nails are short.

7. If you have a pup, a younger dog, or active children in the house, be sure to provide your older dog with a place where he can rest undisturbed. A separate yard or a baby gate inside might be useful when there is more activity around than he can handle.

8. Be sure he has the security of a fenced yard. Older dogs can get disoriented and wander off.

9. Spend twenty minutes of quality time with him every day, giving him a gentle massage, brushing him, and checking him for lumps, fleas, and skin problems.

10. If he's had some obedience training, do a couple of fun five-minute practice sessions with him every day. Give him lots of praise for responding to your commands.

11. Try to maintain a consistent routine and take into account that his bladder and bowel control may not be as good as it used to be. Install a dog door, if necessary, in an easily accessible place, perhaps near his bed.

12. If he's incontinent when he sleeps, lay a sheet of plastic on his bed and cover it with washable absorbent padding.

13. Be aware that he will be less able to tolerate heat and cold, so never leave him in the car when it's even vaguely warm or chilly. Make sure there is plenty of shade and a cozy, draft-free doghouse in his yard. If he gets chilly easily, get a doggy sweater or coat for him to wear.

Why this works: Keeping your dog from getting fat will give his old body and heart less weight to carry around—especially important for dogs with weak hindquarters. A warm bed, which is important throughout his life, will reduce the chance of arthritis, prevent large calluses from forming (particularly on his elbows), and protect his kidneys.

Massage is excellent for keeping him limber and making him feel well loved. Your company will give him peace of mind. He must continue to feel loved, adored, and cared about, and the massage and touching will help him feel special and needed.

Prevention: There is, of course, no prevention for growing old, but the better you take care of your dog, the longer he will live a happy and healthy life. Let him know you love him, and make him as comfortable as possible. A warm, cozy place to rest and sleep, along with your company, care, affection, and common sense will help him stay contented in his old age.

OVEREATING

Problem: My dog is always hungry. She eats like a pig, and she's getting a little plump.

Why your dog is doing this: In the wild, dogs gorged themselves when food was available, because they never knew when they might eat again. This gorging instinct is obviously at work in your dog. Perhaps food was scarce when she was younger.

What to say and do:

1. Have your veterinarian help you determine how much food your dog needs each day to maintain a healthy weight. Divide that amount into two meals a day, one in the morning and one in the evening.

2. Feed your dog a high-quality natural dog food, such as those available in specialty dog food stores, or find out how to prepare healthy meals for her.

3. If your dog looks at you with pleading, starving eyes, steel yourself and ignore her. If you must give in, provide her with non-fattening treats such as raw carrots and broccoli or popcorn (no butter or salt).

4. Make sure your dog is not eating cat food or garbage behind your back.

5. Start her on an exercise program with romps in the park, but go easy on her. Don't suddenly force an out-of-shape dog to go jogging with you.

6. Give her beef knuckle or marrow bones to gnaw on. Remove any clumps of fat from the bones.

Why this works: A high-quality natural diet will provide everything she needs nutritionally, and it may also reduce her cravings. Exercise will burn up accumulated fat and take her mind off of food for a while.

Prevention: Controlling your dog's food intake is totally up to you. Don't feed your dog when she looks at you hungrily and don't let her make you feel guilty (that's the hardest part). Separate your own need to feed her from her need for good health. You are doing her a disservice by keeping her overweight. Discuss this problem with your veterinarian and have her checked for parasites or other physical problems that might be contributing to her big appetite.

See also:
   Begging at mealtime
   Begging for treats

Paper Training. see Housebreaking: Paper Training

Playing Too Exuberantly with Kids

Problem: My dog loves children, but he gets too wild when he plays with them. Sometimes he chases them around and even jumps on them. I'm afraid he'll hurt them.

Why your dog is doing this: Your dog views kids as playmates and plays with them the way he would play with other dogs.

What to say and do:

1. Set your dog up for an ambush. Have your kids, or someone else's, romp around the house noisily. The instant the dog starts to jump or to play too exuberantly, pounce on him with the scruff grip and tell him, "No! Settle down," or "Off! No jumping." Make the correction startling. Then release your grip slowly and ease into a calming neck massage.

2. Then give your dog toys to play with. Let the kids pull a long branch or a knotted length of cloth behind them so that your dog can chase it, or give them a slightly deflated soccer ball to play with.

3. Keep a leash on your dog if he continues to jump on the kids, and use the leash snap to correct him. Use the shaker can, too, if necessary.

4. If your dog continues to chase the children, keep hold of the leash and snap it, using the shaker can at the same time and saying, "Leave it," the instant he lights out after the kids. Then praise him and massage him, but watch closely and be ready to repeat the correction if necessary. Do a quick obedience drill if he still seems fixated on the kids.

5. Repeat this procedure until the dog ignores the kids. Then remove the leash. If he lunges, bellow, "Leave it!" and toss the shaker can at his back end. If you can, grab him, give him the scruff grip, and lecture him firmly: "No chasing! Bad dog!" Then have him sit and ease into a calming massage.

6. When he's good with kids in your house and yard, take him to the park on a long line. If he shows any interest in chasing kids, jumping on them, or playing too wildly with them, correct him before his body is in motion.

Why this works: By consistently correcting your dog, you are discouraging his rambunctious behavior, and by providing suitable toys, you're making sure that the kids are no longer his only toys.

By ambushing him, you're able to correct him the instant he thinks about getting too playful, and you're telling him it's bad to chase and jump, but it's good to stop and sit and be calm.

By consistently making wild behavior unpleasant and by establishing yourself as pack leader with quick obedience drills, you're teaching your dog to think twice about jumping and chasing.

Prevention: Don't leave your dog alone with small children. Teach him some obedience commands and practice them around kids, first indoors and then outside in the yard. Make sure the kids are not inciting the dog's bad behavior. Give them long toys to pull for the dog to play with.

Teach your dog to sit whenever he greets a child. Put him in a sit-stay before and during the hello. Use your left hand to massage and calm him and your right hand to control him with the leash or collar. If he jumps up, tell him, "Off! Stay off!" and snap him down into a sit. Praise him, tell him to stay, and resume the calming massage.

Keep your dog away from children when he's off-leash until he learns to control himself around them, and even then keep the shaker can with you, just in case.

Don't let your kids play tug-of-war with the dog. Instead, teach your dog to retrieve.

See also:
Jumping on me
Retrieving, incomplete

PLAYING WITH OTHER DOGS

Problem: My dog would love to play with other dogs, but I'm not sure how to get him together with them.

Why your dog is doing this: As pack animals, dog lived in extended family groups and had regular contact with other dogs. It's very isolating for dogs to be constantly surrounded by humans and never have a chance to be with their own kind.

What to say and do:

1. Find a suitable playmate for your dog, either by hanging out in the park, by making arrangements with friends, or by putting a sign up at your vet or pet store. Make sure the other dog is friendly and of a similar size, and if your dog is dominant, find a playmate of the opposite sex.

2. If you have a small pup, don't let him play roughly with big, rambunctious dogs—he could get injured. Similarly, if you have a big, loose-bodied puppy from a giant breed, make sure you find him a gentle playmate.

3. Turn the dogs loose together in a fenced area and watch the fun. If their play involves playful wrestling and nipping, as is common, remove their collars to prevent them from getting their jaws caught. Never let dogs wear choke chains while playing, since that kind of slip collar can get caught on a tooth or nail and pulled too tight.

4. If you have small children around, keep them away from the dogs while they are playing; they could get knocked over or trapped between nipping dogs. If the dogs bash into you in play, correct them by bumping them back firmly. This way, they'll get the idea that you are not fun to bash into, and they will leave you alone.

5. When you find a compatible playmate, arrange regular playtimes. Once you are certain the dogs are compatible, consider letting them spend some time alone together. Gradually build up the amount of time they're left alone, making sure their barking doesn't disturb the neighbors.

Why this works: Letting your dog play off-leash with his own species allows him to interact naturally and learn to enjoy other dogs. It is good not only for his physical health but for his mental and emotional health as well.

Prevention: Allow your dog to play with other dogs from puppyhood so as to prevent his innocent excitement from turning into intense frustration that could lead to aggression later on. As he plays, he will acquire canine social skills and be less likely to become aggressive.

See also:
New dog, introducing

POSSESSIVENESS OF FOOD

Problem: My dog growls menacingly at us if we try to take food away from him. This is a real problem if he picks up something dangerous, such as a chicken bone.

Why your dog is doing this: Your dog does not respect you as his pack leader and is warning you to back off, just as he would warn away an underling in his pack.

What to say and do:

1. Do not try to take the food out of your dog's mouth; you could get bitten.

2. Consult with a professional trainer who is experienced in dealing with aggression.

3. Put your dog through a formal obedience training course, which will elevate you to pack leader.

4. Once he's well acquainted with the sit-stay command, put him on-leash and drop some food several feet away from him while he maintains the sit-stay. If he makes a dive for the food tell him, "Leave it!" snap the leash, and use the spray bottle. Then praise him, saying, "Good to leave it!" Command him to sit again and praise him; then have him stay while you pick up the food. Release him and play with him. Repeat this exercise, including the playtime, several times in a row every day until he sits and stays when you drop food on the floor and waits for you to pick it up.

5. Hand-feed your dog his meals, chunk by chunk, so he will see that you are the hand that feeds him.

6. If he continues to growl at you when you try to take his food away, you must seek professional help.

7. Spend a half hour each day giving your dog a calming massage, so that you and your dog can connect in a calm, loving way.

Why this works: The obedience training will teach your dog to respect you and will help him form a working relationship with you; it should also change his mind about his status in the pack.

Prevention: Early puppy handling and gentle obedience work will teach your pup that you are the pack leader and, as such, have undisputed access to his body and mouth.

If your dog is growling at you, don't try to take the food away. Hire a professional trainer.

POSSESSIVENESS OF OBJECTS

Problem: My dog sometimes grabs an object and runs off with it. She actually snaps at us when we try to take it away from her.

Why your dog is doing this: In the past, your dog may have been treated harshly for grabbing forbidden objects. She thinks you're going to hurt her, so she growls and snaps in self-defense. Also, if you did not give her anything to play with, she may have been forced to find her own "toys." And if you ever played tug-of-war with her, you unknowingly caused this behavior.

Some dogs steal things just for the fun of being chased by their owners.

Whatever the reason for your dog's thievery, the procedure for solving this problem is always the same.

What to say and do:

1. Give your dog plenty of acceptable toys.

2. Enroll in a formal obedience program so that she will learn to respect you and take you seriously.

3. Attach a leash to her buckle collar in the house when you are home to make her easier to catch. Use a leash without a loop on the end, so it won't catch on anything and perhaps strangle her.

4. If she picks up a forbidden object, do not yell at her or grab her. Just say, "You silly girl, what have you got this time?" She will look shocked at first, because this is such a different response. Invite her over to you with lots of sweet talk, using the leash if necessary. Ask her to sit, and then praise her. If she does not snap at you, gently take it from her and praise her.

5. If she is defensive, then offer her a trade instead. Ask her, "Do you want to trade this cookie for my underwear?" Let her sniff the cookie, and when she drops your underwear, praise her and give her the treat.

6. Repeat the correct sequence whenever she picks up a forbidden object.

7. When you're around, leave some forbidden objects on the floor. If she starts to grab one, correct her firmly before she gets her mouth on it. Say, "Leave it!" and, if necessary, back up your voice with the spray bottle. Then happily give her an acceptable toy.

8. If the problem continues, ask a professional trainer to help you retrain your dog.

Why this works: By showing no anger, you give your dog no reason to be afraid of your approach, since she knows she's not going to get yelled at, grabbed, or corrected. When her fear subsides, she will stop snapping. Providing her with her own toys gives her something acceptable to chew on, so she won't steal your things. And the obedience work and calming massage provide her with quality time and attention.

Prevention: Don't be harsh with your dog when she steals your things. Don't hit her, grab her, or agitate her. Use the leash gently to get her out of corners, talking to her happily.

Never play tug-of-war with a dog. Calmly teach the dog to fetch instead. Let her know that if she takes something inappropriate, she can bring it to you and get praised.

Spend twenty minutes a day giving her a calming massage so you can have some quiet time together.

Provide acceptable toys as soon as she comes to live with you.

REFUSING TO LISTEN TO YOU. SEE IGNORING YOU

REFUSING TO PLAY WITH THE NEW PUPPY

Problem: Our older dog is not interested in playing with our new puppy.

Why your dog is doing this: Your older dog is probably disgusted that you have brought in a new pup. By ignoring her, he is teaching her that he is the pack leader and must be respected. He may also view the pup as an intruder in his household.

What to say and do:

1. Let your older dog make up to your pup in his own sweet time. If he growls to keep her away, that's okay. He may start to play with her once he sees that she accepts his terms.

2. Take them for walks together so your older dog can be the knowledgeable leader, with the pup following curiously and respectfully.

3. Give your older dog calming massage sessions and have someone else sit nearby and massage the puppy. Always talk to your dog happily about the new pup.

4. Play with your dogs in the yard or in the house. Provide a long toy, such as an old tablecloth tied in knots, and encourage your pup to chase the end of it as you drag it around.

5. Speak happily to your older dog when you are petting him and the pup comes up. Let him see that the presence of the puppy means that fun things will happen.

6. Give him a place he can retreat to where the pup can't bug him. A separate puppy pen in your yard will allow them to be separated but close enough to get acquainted; crates and baby gates will do for inside.

7. Review your older dog's obedience training to remind him that you are the top dog in the pack; it will also be a form of quality time spent with him. When you are training the pup, let your older dog watch. He will feel pleased to see that you are getting that silly, ill-mannered pup under control!

Why this works: Letting your dog maintain his space and allowing the two of them to work out their relationship on their own is nature's way: in a wild pack, the older dogs set limits for the pups and teach them respect. Taking walks together will help your dog view the pup as part of his pack. The calming massage and play sessions will help him drop his defenses and warm up to the pup.

Prevention: Don't force the pup onto your dog. Don't leave them alone together until they have become good friends. Make sure your older dog gets to spend one-on-one time with you, as he did before the pup's arrival.

Provide your pup with her own water, food bowl, and toys. Feed your dogs separately so there is no competition or food-stealing.

See also:
New dog, introducing

RETRIEVING, INCOMPLETE

Problem: When we throw something for our dog to retrieve, he runs after it and picks it up, but then he trots off with it and plays keep-away when we try to take it from him.

Why young dog is doing this: If you have ever grabbed a toy from him, he has learned to hang back so you won't snatch things away from him. This has turned into a new game of chase-me-to-get-it.

What to say and do:

1. Sit on a rug near an uncarpeted area, and toss one of your dog's favorite toys onto the bare floor, saying, "Go get it!" As soon as he picks it up, say, "Good boy! Bring it!" and pat the rug next to you, keeping your hands low and near your body. Praise him enthusiastically if he comes to you. If he doesn't come, put a leash on him and tug him to you gently.

2. When he returns to you, don't grab the object. Pet your dog, but not on his head or he'll think you're going to grab his toy. Instead, rub his backside or invite him into your lap, if he fits. Let him hang out next to you and play with or chew on his toy for a minute, and then take it from him. Repeat this procedure until he catches on. Then move this exercise outdoors.

Why this works: When your dog sees that he can play with his toy while lying next to you and getting petted, he'll come back to you after fetching whatever you have thrown.

Prevention: Never play tug-of-war. It teaches your dog to growl and hang on to an object.

When your dog returns to you with the toy you've thrown, never lunge at him or make a grab for the toy. This will only teach him to avoid you. Don't play chase games with him when he has a toy in his mouth.

Never get angry with him if he doesn't pick up the toy. Talk happily to him while showing him where it went and encourage him to pick it up on his own. Then dash back to your base camp and play with him there. Stop the retrieving game before he gets tired of it, so he will look forward to playing it with you again.

ROAMING

Problem: Whenever we let our dog out, he roams all over the neighborhood. We're afraid something terrible will happen to him.

Why your dog is doing this: Dogs like to roam and explore new territory, just as they would in the wild.

What to say and do:

1. *Never let your dog run loose outside without supervision.*

2. Take him outside with you only when you can pay attention to him and play with him or train him. Practice his obedience training in your front yard, and be positive, upbeat, and entertaining.

3. Surprise your dog by stationing yourself along his escape path. When he trots toward you, chase him home by using the shaker can or hitting the ground with a tree branch and yelling, "Go home!" When he's back on his property, praise him.

4. Get your male dog neutered. Intact males tend to roam.

5. Tell your neighbors not to welcome him when he comes over. Have them send him home instead.

Why this works: Your dog will be more inclined to stay home if you are actively involved with him whenever he is loose outside. The obedience training helps him to see you as his pack leader. When he begins to view your home as a place that's fun, he'll want to stay there.

By ambushing him when he leaves, you show him that roaming makes you mad.

Prevention: Never leave your dog outside in an unfenced area. Monitor him whenever he is outside off-leash, and provide him with a securely fenced yard so that he'll form the habit of staying home. If you do see him start to slip away, give him a sharp verbal reminder to stay home.

Start obedience training at a young age to establish control and to strengthen the bond between you and your dog.

See also:
Hard to catch
Off-leash misbehavior
Running away

Running Away

Problem: My dog runs away every chance he gets. I can't bear to think about him being lost, stolen, or killed.

Why your dog is doing this: Your dog may be unhappy with his home life. Is he being abused or neglected? Is he bored? Maybe he's not getting enough exercise, playtime, and attention. Also, as pack animals, dogs need to form a strong bond with their pack family. If he doesn't feel a special connection with you, he won't feel that he belongs with you, and he will run away, hoping to find a better life elsewhere.

What to say and do:

1. Make your dog feel that he is a special and important member of your home. If he is an outside dog—and that, by the way, is a terrible life for a dog—bring him in, teach him some house manners, and let him spend time with you inside. Let him sleep indoors at night, preferably in your bedroom, where he can be close to you and hear you breathing and tossing about.

2. Practice his obedience training. This will increase his respect for you as his pack leader, and strengthen the bond between you. Practice the commands both indoors and outdoors, especially the come command.

3. Provide him with toys and things to gnaw on, and be a fun companion to him.

4. Feed your dog two hearty, tasty meals a day—one in the morning and another in the evening. This will make him want to stay around for the next meal. Feeding him at specific times, as opposed to leaving the food down all the time, helps him see you as the pack leader who brings home the meat.

5. Spend a half hour a day giving him a calming massage in a quiet place in the house.

6. Take him on long walks and outings in the car with you; always bring some treats and a favorite toy. Let him romp around on a long line.

7. If he's still intact, get him neutered so that he'll be less interested in cruising.

Why this works: By incorporating your dog into your life, you become his pack leader. If your heart is open to him and you show him love, care, and affection, he will never want to leave your side.

Prevention: Here's a general rule: Unhappy dogs run away. Don't let your dog pine away alone in the yard day after miserable day. Dogs are pack animals and need companionship. If you provide companionship for your dog, along with good food, exercise, and a cozy bed next to yours, he will not run away and look for a better life elsewhere.

Neuter or spay your dog. If he has been tied up outside, provide him with a fenced yard instead, so he can play without being anchored down. Give him a sandbox to dig in and a wading pool in the summer.

See also:
Bolting out of the house
Hard to catch
Off-leash misbehavior
Roaming

SCRATCHING AT THE DOOR

Problem: Whenever my dog wants to come in the house, he scratches on the door. The screen door is ripped, and there are giant claw marks on the wooden door.

Why your dog is doing this: Your dog has probably been let in the house when he scratched on the door before, and since this worked for him in the past, he assumes it will work for him again.

What to say and do:

1. When he scratches on the door, open it abruptly, and gently but firmly bump him with it. Don't hurt him; just startle him. At the same time, tell him in a sharp voice: "No! Quit that!" Close the door immediately and wait. If he scratches again, repeat the correction. If the door opens inward, use the shaker can or spray bottle to startle and correct him.

2. After you correct him, wait until he stays quiet for three to five minutes. Then praise him calmly as you open the door and let him in. Increase the amount of time he remains outside quietly after being corrected before you let him in. Eventually he will learn to wait outside until you decide he can come in.

Why this works: If he is corrected instead of being let in, he will learn not to scratch the door.

Prevention: Never let your dog in when he scratches. Make him sit patiently until you open the door. Do not let him think he can control you, but don't forget he's outside—and be careful not to neglect him.

If your dog is trustworthy in the house, install a dog door so he can come and go as he pleases. Provide him with a cozy doghouse outside, and make his yard a fun place by giving him toys to play with and things to gnaw on.

Take care that he does not spend all his time isolated in the yard, and be sure to incorporate him into your life. Give him house time, let him sleep indoors at night, play with him, train him, take him on outings, and spend quiet time together. And if the habit of scratching your door is simply too tough to change, you can protect your doors by installing a panel of sheet metal or grating.

See also:
Dog door, fear of

SHYNESS

Problem: My dog is very timid about meeting new people. She wants to greet them and is curious, but she's painfully shy.

Why your dog is doing this: Your dog isn't sure that new people will be kind to her. Some pups are born shy, and if they don't get special handling as puppies, their shyness will persist. Even an outgoing pup will become shy if she doesn't have pleasant experiences with new people and places as she grows up. Dogs who have been abused can become fearful to the point of snapping if someone comes too close to them.

What to say and do:

1. Greet people cheerfully yourself. Your dog will sense your comfort, and she will be comfortable too.

2. Ask the stranger to squat down to your dog's level while you do so yourself. Have him hold out his hand to her, keeping it low and beneath the level of her head. Never reach for her from the top. Let her sniff the person while he holds perfectly still. Talk happily to her the whole time: "Say hello, Missy." If she still seems worried, give the stranger some treats to feed her, or take the person's hand and let your dog sniff both hands together.

3. If she doesn't like the stranger making the first move, let her sniff him while he stands or squats and totally ignores her. After she has sniffed him, she will relax a little.

4. Spend a minimum of twenty minutes a day giving her a calming massage to help ease her tension and fear. Use this calming work to help her stay relaxed when she meets people.

5. Take your dog on walks with another friendly, confident dog that your dog likes. Go to parks and let her meet all the dogs and people.

6. Enroll her in an obedience class, so she can get socialized around other dogs and people and learn some basic commands, which will build up her confidence.

Why this works: Your friendliness lets her see that you are not at all scared. Squatting down to her level makes people seem smaller, which helps her feel less threatened. Allowing her to sniff someone who is ignoring her gives her time to familiarize herself with the stranger and not feel pressured or cornered.

Prevention: Early and continuous socialization with proper handling as a pup will help your dog learn that people are fun to meet.

Don't let anyone tease your dog, corner her, or threaten her in any way.

See also:
Abused dog
Hand-shyness
Nervousness

SNAPPING AT ADULTS

Problem: My dog sometimes snaps at adults who try to pet her.

Why your dog is doing this: The way a nervous or shy dog is approached by adults can make the dog feel threatened. By making sudden moves, coming on too fast, speaking too loud, or towering above the dog, an adult can frighten your dog, and she may snap.

Some dogs just don't want to be bothered by certain people. Like humans, dogs can sense when someone is not quite trustworthy. Your dog's way of telling these people to leave her alone is to snap at them.

What to say and do:

1. Snapping must be considered an aggressive act, even though your dog is probably doing it out of fear. Get a qualified and compassionate trainer to help your dog overcome this problem.

2. When someone wants to say hello to your dog, greet that person in a very happy, upbeat voice, so she will see that you are relaxed and friendly.

3. Have some treats handy for the other person to feed your dog. If she won't accept food from a stranger, give the treats to her yourself. While you continue to talk happily, both of you should squat down. Take hold of the other person's hand, and encourage your dog to sniff both hands together. Massage her neck with your free hand. Make sure the newcomer keeps his hands low and avoids any quick, startling movements. Stop petting the dog before she backs away on her own.

4. If she does make an attempt to snap, correct her with the leash snap or use the scruff grip with your massage hand. Be firm enough to let her know you don't like her behavior; then return to the massage.

Why this works: By correcting your dog for snapping, you're showing her that you won't tolerate this behavior. If she respects you as the pack leader, she will want to please you. A foundation in obedience training will help build her confidence and teach her to respect your wishes. The calming massage will help her relax and be less afraid.

Prevention: Spend a minimum of twenty minutes a day giving her a calming massage. If she is fearful, there will be tension in her body, and the massage will relax her.

Make sure no one teases or startles her. Don't force your dog to be petted. If it takes her a while to feel comfortable around new people, that's fine. Let her warm up to them at her own pace. If she's resting, instruct people to leave her alone.

Monitor your dog carefully if there are children around and she doesn't like kids.

Never leave your dog tied up in front of a store or anywhere else if you are not with her. This is cruel and she may feel helpless, abandoned, or cornered and could bite someone.

Early socialization of puppies will prevent a snapping problem from developing. Enroll your dog in an obedience class for the training and socializing it offers. If necessary, seek the help of a private trainer.

See also:
Abused dog
Shyness

SNAPPING AT OTHER PEOPLE'S CHILDREN

Problem: My dog does not like to be approached and touched by kids and will often snap at them.

Why your dog is doing this: If your dog was not adequately socialized with kind children as she grew up, she may view kids as hurtful or annoying. Dogs who have been teased by children or disturbed while they are resting will view children as tormentors.

What to say and do:

1. If your dog tends to snap at children, get the help of a professional trainer. Snapping can lead to biting and must be taken seriously.

2. Whenever kids approach your dog, have them stop several feet away. Talk happily to them, making it obvious to your dog that you think these small humans are great. Carry treats with you on all your walks and have the kids place a few on the ground for her to pick up.

3. If your dog has a favorite retrieving toy, let the kids throw it for her, but take it back from her yourself. A child reaching toward her face could cause your dog to snap at them. Hand it back to the kids to toss again.

4. Don't force your dog to endure being petted by children. If she starts to relax and enjoy them, she will in time approach them to be petted in her own way, on her own time.

5. If she does snap at the kids, correct her with the scruff grip instantly, glare into her eyes, and lecture her in a very serious low voice. Then put her through two to three minutes of firm obedience work and demand that she pay attention to you. Sound disgusted. Soften up slowly and give her low-key praise and a calming massage to her neck and head while you visit with the kids, who should be far enough back so that your dog does not feel cornered.

6. After your dog has settled down, happily offer her a treat and give the kids some treats to drop on the ground for her as well. Be cheerful and upbeat to help everyone relax, including your dog. This way, she sees that the incident is over and that the kids are still around and are not bad company at a distance, especially if they are handing out treats. If you drag her off and keep her away from the kids, she will never have a chance to change her mind about them.

7. If these methods do not work, protect your dog from kids and vice versa, and find a professional trainer to help you solve this problem.

Why this works: If your dog consistently experiences children as fun and friendly, she may decide that they are fun to be around.

Prevention: Do not leave your dog unattended when there are children around or when they might show up. Never tie your dog up in the front yard, or anyplace else, and never let her run loose while you are preoccupied.

If your dog doesn't like children, you must tell the kids to stay away from her for their own safety.

Make sure your dog is never cornered, teased, or startled by kids. Early and continuous socialization around kids will ensure your pup grows up enjoying their company and even looks forward to seeing them.

Spend a minimum of twenty minutes a day giving her a calming massage. Get her used to relaxing easily and quickly under your hands. Then, when you have her in situations where she feels anxious, she'll calm down quickly under your familiar hands.

Enroll your dog in a structured obedience program. Find a specialized class or hire a private trainer to deal with the specific problem of snapping at children.

See also:
Abused dog
Shyness

SNAPPING AT YOUR CHILDREN

Problem: My dog snaps at my children if they try to hug her when she is resting.

Why your dog is doing this: Like many people, your dog dislikes being bothered when she's resting.

What to say and do:

1. Tell your kids that the dog likes to rest undisturbed, just as they do.

2. If you catch your dog snapping, scold her firmly: "Don't you snap!" and if necessary, do the scruff grip. Then put her through a two- to three-minute obedience drill and end with a calming massage.

3. If your dog is resting but not asleep, you may let your child give her a treat instead of a hug. This way she experiences the approach of your child not as an intrusion but as something to enjoy.

4. If you are petting your resting dog and your child comes over, welcome the child warmly. Give your dog a calming massage while your child visits quietly with both of you.

5. Let your dog and your child spend supervised time together doing things they both enjoy such as playing fetch or romping in the park. Let your child help you feed the dog, so your dog sees your child as someone who provides her with food.

Why this works: When your resting dog realizes your child is approaching with a treat in hand, she actually begins to look forward to this visit. Giving your dog a place to rest where she will be left alone will help her tolerate the kids when she is awake.

Prevention: Make sure your dog has a place to rest undisturbed. Teach your kids and their friends to leave the dog alone when she's there.

Teach your children not to put their faces directly in the dog's face; this can be viewed by your dog as more intrusive than just a pat, and the chances of your child being bitten are higher.

Make sure that your kids treat the dog with the utmost respect—the way they would want to be treated. Warn them that if they continue to pester your dog, they might get bitten.

SNIFFING PEOPLE

Problem: Whenever my dog meets new people, she wants to sniff them carefully—all over, even in the crotch area.

Why your dog is doing this: Your dog takes in information about all sorts of things through her powerful sense of smell. When dogs greet one another, they smell each other thoroughly, sniffing the genitals to identify each other's sex. Your dog sniffs people for the same reason.

What to say and do:

1. Let your dog sniff people's hands, legs, feet, and shoes. If some people are uncomfortable with the sniffing, too bad for them! Explain to your friends that this is how your dog familiarizes herself with new people and reacquaints herself with friends. Let her sniff them briefly and then have her sit next to you.

2. But if she closes in on your crotch or anyone else's, give her a quick, firm rap on the nose or the rump and tell her "No!" Do this whether she approaches from the front or the back, and do it every time she tries. You must startle her in order to teach her not to do it again.

3. Teach your dog to sit when she meets people. If she still tries to ram her head into someone's crotch, correct her with the butt tap or, if she's on-leash, give her a leash snap. If she persists, use the scruff grip, give her a firm shake or two, and glare at her while you say, "No! Leave it!"

Why this works: By letting your dog check people out with her nose, you allow her to learn that they are not threatening. This is especially important if your dog is shy, has been abused, has a tendency to snap, or is dominant.

By giving her a quick bop, you are doing much the same thing that another dog would do to her if she got too personal too soon.

Prevention: If it is important that your dog not sniff a certain person, simply say, "No!" and have her sit and stay by your side. Give her a brief calming massage to keep her still and occupied.

Never let your dog sniff your crotch or anyone else's.

Keep her out of the wastebasket in the bathroom, because she'll be attracted to tissues, feminine napkins, and the like. If she bothers a toddler in diapers or raids the garbage for dirty diapers, correct her firmly.

Don't let your dog hump your leg or anyone else's.

Obedience-train her so she'll understand her place in the pack and respect you and others.

STAIRS, FEAR OF

Problem: My dog is afraid of stairways, especially if she's at the top. She just refuses to go down them. I'm getting tired of carrying her around.

Why your dog is doing this: From your dog's perspective, the top of the stairway is as scary as the edge of a cliff. If she's little, she can't see the steps—only what looks like a drop-off. If she's a big dog, perhaps she had a bad experience with stairs; she could have tripped, fallen, or been pushed.

What to say and do:

1. If your stairs are slippery, firmly secure strips of carpet to them. Put carpeting on the landings, both top and bottom. Put some traction strips on the outside stairs for safety and security. This way they won't be slippery, and she'll feel safer on them.

2. If your dog is afraid to go down the stairs, carry her down, set her on the bottom step, and pet her until she relaxes, slowly encouraging her to jump to the floor. Use treats if necessary, scattering them on the step so she will relax, sniff around, and eat them. Then put the treats on the floor just below the step. If she's still too scared to hop to the floor, very gently and carefully lower her front legs to the floor and she should follow with her back legs. As you are doing this, be sure to encourage her verbally.

3. Repeat this exercise until she hops from the bottom step to the floor easily. Then place her on the second step and use treats again to help her hop to the bottom step and then to the floor. Work your way up the stairs as she gains confidence. Eventually she will descend the stairs on her own.

4. If your dog is afraid to go up the stairs, put her on the step next to the top and use treats and encouraging words to get her to hop up to the landing. Work your way up, stair by stair, the same way you would entice her to go down.

5. If she's still afraid of the stairs in general, spend time with her on the stairs, just hanging out, until she relaxes. Feed her treats, pet her, give her a massage, and let her get comfortable on one step at a time.

6. For open stairways that have no risers, tack wooden slats across the openings so that she can't see down or slip through. Practice the same procedure—going up and down in the same way you did with the inside stairs.

Why this works: By showing your dog that the stairs are simply individual ledges to be explored you'll give her the confidence to go up and down them.

Prevention: Make sure there is good traction so you pup doesn't fall down slippery stairs.

Practice on low, wide steps—a stoop, for instance—before tackling a steeper stairway.

STEALING FOOD FROM CHILDREN

Problem: Whenever my children walk around with food, my dog snatches it from their hands.

Why your dog is doing this: Dogs are scavengers; if they see an opportunity to grab a treat, they'll seize it. Also, your dog doesn't respect the kids, so he'll simply take their food.

What to say and do:

1. Leash your dog and set up an ambush by giving your kids some treats. The second your dog makes a move for the treats, correct her by snapping the leash and if necessary use the spray bottle or shaker can and say firmly, "No!" Praise her calmly for moving away from the food. Watch her, and if she attempts another food theft, correct her again.

2. With the dog off-leash, seat the kids at a low table and give them something to munch on. When your dog tries to steal from them, toss the shaker can at her rump and startle her or get her in a scruff grip and haul her away from the table, telling her, "No! Leave it!" If she returns, shoo her away noisily.

3. Teach the kids not to give the dog their food.

Why this works: By startling your dog before she gets the food in her mouth, you are telling her not to even think about stealing from your children. Your quick, strong words and actions help your dog see you as the top dog protecting her young from having their food stolen.

Prevention: Keep your dog away from the cooking area during food preparation so she'll learn that people food is off-limits. Don't confine her in the kitchen where countertops and garbage are available for raiding.

Show her, through obedience training, that you are the boss so that she will respect you.

Teach your children not to offer her any of their food. Have dog treats they can give to her in her bowl.

If you are feeding her one meal a day, switch to two, so she doesn't get as hungry between meals.

STEALING FOOD OFF COUNTERS

Problem: If I turn my back for even a second, my dog will grab food off the counter or table. He's a terrible thief!

Why your dog is doing this: Dogs are scavengers. In the wild, they scavenged leftovers from other carcasses and from human camps. If your dog doesn't respect you as his pack leader, he will steal from your food supply.

What to say and do:

1. Don't confine your dog in the kitchen unattended. Leave him where there is no food to tempt him.

2. Catch him in the act by setting up an ambush. Leave some tasty morsel near the edge of the counter and casually go about your business. Wait until your dog makes a grab for the food. Then startle him by grabbing his scruff, using the shaker can, and yelling, "No! Leave it! Shame on you! Don't you ever steal my food!" Push him back to the floor and angrily tell him, "Go away!"

3. If he looks humbled, you got your message across. Thank him in a soft yet cautioning voice, "Good boy to leave my food alone." Dogs respond to negative correction as well as positive reinforcement. He will see that you get mad when he steals food, and that you're happy when he leaves it alone.

4. Repeat this lesson as many times as you need to over a period of days. Leave the kitchen, observe your dog drooling over the hot dog you've left on the counter, and ambush him if necessary.

5. You can coat food in Tabasco sauce and add a little cayenne to deter a determined dog from stealing, but this won't work if your dog likes it hot!

6. Inflated balloons taped to the edge of the counter may repel him if he's afraid they'll pop. To prepare for this, blow up a balloon and sit on the floor. When he wanders over to check it out, pop it in his face with a pin.

7. Practice obedience training in the kitchen to remind your dog to listen to you there.

8. To see if your dog is up to no good in your absence, sprinkle talcum powder on the edge of the countertop so you'll be able to detect any telltale paw prints!

Why this works: Correcting your dog as he leaps for the food—before he gets it in his mouth—is the only way to teach him not to steal. Correcting him after the fact won't work. The obedience training will help elevate you to pack leader, so he will want to please you and will take your corrections seriously.

Prevention: Don't leave your dog alone in the kitchen, and don't feed your dog treats from the counter. Put them in his bowl so that he will not look to the counter or the table for food.

Obedience-train your dog so that he will respect you and take your corrections seriously. Practice the training in the kitchen, but shoo him away firmly when you are preparing food. Let him know that your food is not for him.

If you are feeding him one meal a day, switch to two so he won't get as hungry between meals. Make sure his diet is tasty and nutritionally complete.

STEALING OBJECTS. SEE POSSESSIVENESS OF OBJECTS

STUBBORNNESS. SEE IGNORING YOU

TODDLERS. SEE BABIES, TODDLERS

TOILET, DRINKING FROM

Problem: My dog loves to drink from the toilet. The slobber on the seat is disgusting!

Why your dog is doing this: The toilet is a guaranteed source of cool, clean water. If his water bowl is too small, filled with dirty or lukewarm water, or inconveniently placed, he will head for the toilet.

What to say and do:

1. The simplest solution—though not the easiest for everyone to remember—is to keep the toilet lid down.

2. Provide your dog with a big bucket of water that you keep one-half to three-quarters full (when he drinks, most of his slobber will go back in the bucket). Keep it in a convenient place in the house where you won't mind a bit of slobber on the floor.

3. When you hear him drinking from the toilet, sneak in behind him and drop the lid gently on his head. Just startle him; don't hurt him. Order him out of the bathroom and guide him cheerfully to his new big bucket.

Why this works: If everyone remembers to put the lid down, your dog won't patronize his favorite watering hole.

Prevention: Alway provide lots of fresh water for your dog to drink.

When he's a puppy, if you see him begin to drink from the toilet, discourage him immediately. This will get him into the habit of drinking from his own water bowl. Make sure to clean out his water bowl or bucket regularly to remove slime and debris.

TRAVELING BY AIRPLANE

Problem: My dog will be traveling on an airplane soon. What can I do to prepare him for the journey so he'll be comfortable and not afraid?

What to say and do:

1. Your dog will travel in an airline crate, so buy the crate several weeks in advance to get him used to it.

2. Once he is comfortable, start getting him used to being in the crate when it's being moved around. If the crate is small enough to pick up, carry it around a bit. If it is too heavy to lift, slide it around the floor gently. As you do, reassure your dog: "It's okay!"

3. When he's comfortable being in a moving crate, take him for car rides in the crate so he can get used to the motion and noise.

4. To prepare your dog for the loud noise of the airplane, play a tape of an airplane or a thunderstorm—softly at first and then louder as he adjusts—so he can get used to those noises gradually. Play the tape while he is loose in the house and, when he's used to that, while he's in the crate.

5. If he is frightened during these preparations, ask your veterinarian about a sedative to give the dog before the flight. Perhaps a holistic veterinarian can give you a natural remedy to calm your dog.

6. If your dog is on the flight with you and is traveling in the cargo hold, pass a message to the captain that your dog is aboard and ask that a close eye be kept on the temperature and pressure gauges. The cargo hold is kept the same as the passenger section, but it's a good idea to make sure that someone in authority knows your precious cargo is on board.

7. Prior to flying, withhold food for six hours and water for two. Be sure your dog has had a chance to relieve himself before entering the crate.

8. Place soft, absorbent bedding in the crate and give him a toy to chew on. Attach the crate's water tray—empty, of course—to the inside of the door so that the airport staff can fill it if your dog gets held up waiting for a flight.

Why this works: Getting your dog used to the crate prior to shipping gives him time to see the crate as a safe den. If he does get scared on the plane, the familiarity of the crate will help him feel protected and secure.

Prevention: Allow plenty of time at the airport. This will help both you and your dog stay calm.

Book a nonstop flight if possible, since plane changes can lead to a mixup. If there are transfers, leave plenty of time between flights to ensure your dog will make it to the connecting flight. Nonstop flights will also keep your dog from sitting in the cargo hold, which is not heated or cooled when the airplane is on the ground. To avoid temperature extremes, try to ship your dog at night in the summer and during the day in the winter.

Securely attach to the crate the address and phone number of your home and your destination. Include your flight number and emergency phone numbers for you and someone else who knows your dog. Keep an ID tag on your dog's collar with your home address and telephone number. If you are going to be staying at your destination for any length of time, get an ID tag made for the new location as well.

Make sure your dog is up-to-date on his vaccinations and that you have the veterinary certificates with you. Check with your vet to see if your dog needs to be put on any special medication, such as heartworm medicine, prior to his arrival at his new destination. Check with the airlines to see if a health certificate is required before flying.

See also:
Crate training

TRAVELING BY CAR

Problem: I am going to take a road trip with my new dog, who is not a happy traveler, and I want to make sure she has a good time too.

Why your dog is doing this: Car travel can be stressful for dogs. If her diet is off and her exercise is limited, she could have digestive upsets. If she's not used to the car and finds herself in it for endless hours, she might become restless, depressed, or anxious.

What to say and do:

1. Don't let your dog poke her head out the car window. Grit, insects, and other flying objects could damage her eyes, ears, or mouth.

2. Bring toys for her to play with and things to gnaw on. Stop periodically so she can relieve herself. Look for places to exercise her a couple of times a day—open fields, woods, or expansive beaches. If she is not trustworthy off-leash, bring along a 50- to 75-foot cord, so she can stretch her legs and romp.

3. Wherever you stay, make sure there is nothing poisonous that your dog can get into. Backyards, farmyards, or motel landscaping can contain lethal poisons such as slug bait and rat poison. Always ask and check. Be careful of antifreeze that may have leaked onto a driveway.

4. Take along a good supply of poop bags, and always clean up after your dog.

5. Be careful about letting a young puppy relieve herself at highway rest stops. Dogs from all over the country use them, and your pup could pick up a serious parasite or virus. Try to find open spaces not frequented by other dogs.

6. If you are traveling in a hot climate, keep a bowl of water available for your dog in the car. There are water bowls just for this purpose, with lids on them that allow a drink but not spillage. The mist from a spray bottle will help your dog cool down. Spray her all over, including her belly.

7. If you are traveling in a cold climate and your dog is not well coated, make sure she stays warm. Put a warm dog coat on her, if necessary.

8. Make sure the sun is not beating down on her while you're driving, especially if she's in the back of a station wagon. If it's hot out, or even warm, don't leave your dog in the car. A car can reach a lethal temperature in a very short time, even with the windows rolled down *and even on an overcast day.* Be very careful, or you may come back to a dead dog.

Why this works: Preparing your dog for a car trip by crate-training her and teaching her some obedience commands, can ensure that you will have the control over her that you need to keep her safe in strange places. Regular meals and adequate exercise will keep her relaxed and keep her stomach and bowels healthy. Researching places that accept dogs will keep you both comfortable and safe at night. Traveling with a well-mannered dog is a joy, and you will find that your dog will help you meet people you wouldn't ordinarily get a chance to meet.

Prevention: Take your dog for a veterinary checkup well before the trip. Find out about any diseases or harmful parasites that might be prevalent where you are going. Make sure she is up-to-date with her vaccinations, and take her veterinary certificates along with you. If she is on any special medications, take a supply and a backup prescription.

Make sure your dog wears an identification tag with your address and phone number and her license number on her collar. If you will be staying in one place for even a short while, get a temporary tag (available at pet stores) on which you can write your vacation address.

Practice obedience commands around the car. Make sure she will not get in or out of the car until you tell her it's okay. Be certain that she will respond quickly to the down command in case, for example, you have to change lanes and she is blocking your view. If she has no training, teach her a few commands, especially sit, sit-stay, and down.

Get her used to the car prior to your trip. Short, enjoyable outings will help her see the car as a fun place to be.

Get her used to a crate before your journey, and take her crate along. She will feel more secure in strange places if she has her crate to sleep in, and it will give you a safe place to leave her when you visit friends or stay in hotels. This way she can't get herself into trouble. The crate can also serve as a cozy bed for her if you are traveling in a van. If you can't take the crate along, take some familiar comfortable bedding.

Take plenty of her special food, in case you can't find it where you are going. A sudden change in diet may lead to an upset stomach and diarrhea.

Take along a first-aid kid. Ask your veterinarian to supply you with a few essential items.

If you are planning to stay in hotels, there is a directory available that lists dog-friendly places. Check with your local bookstore or auto club.

See also:

Barking in the car
Bolting from the car
Car, fear of
Carsickness
Crate training

TYING UP

Problem: My dog leaps, barks, and pulls on the leash whenever I tie her up.

Why your dog is doing this: If your dog is insecure, she will feel abandoned when separated from you, especially in unfamiliar places. Her leaping about is her attempt to free herself; she cries in the hope of bringing you back to her.

What to say and do:

1. Practice tying her up on a 6-foot leash to something solid inside the house. Give her chew toys and a soft blanket to lie on. Don't use a choke chain, but make certain her regular collar is snug so she can't slip out of it. If she acts up, quickly correct her either verbally or with the leash snap, shaker can, or spray bottle. If she settles down for a few minutes and accepts being tethered, praise her, using slow hands and a calm voice. Let her off her leash. Repeat the exercise, increasing the amount of time she remains tied up.

2. Tie her up in different places around the house until she calmly accepts it. Tether her outside while you putter about the yard nearby. Correct her firmly the instant she acts up.

3. When she accepts being tied up at home, inside and out, practice in front of the corner store. Don't go out of her sight until she's relaxed and quiet with you in view. Then go inside the store and observe her, making certain she doesn't see you, for a minute or two. Return to her immediately and correct her if she starts barking or leaping; the spray bottle works nicely in public.

4. If she must be tethered in the yard, install a cable system for her that is strung overhead between two sturdy objects. An 8- to 10-foot line with swivels in it can be attached to the cable and run down to her collar. This will allow her more exercise and freedom than being tied to a stake, but is not nearly as satisfying for her as total freedom inside a fenced yard. *Never use a choke or slip collar with this device;* either one can put her in danger of becoming tangled or even hanging herself.

Why this works: Starting your dog on short increments of being tied up lets her know immediately that staying quiet is what pleases you. Building on that success and tethering her in different locations for short periods lets her know that you expect her to remain calm wherever you put her. Teaching her in a structured way also allows you to correct her the instant she acts up, before she gets herself in a frenzy.

Prevention: Dogs weren't put on this earth to live out their lives tied to a stake in the backyard. Make sure you aren't neglecting your dog. Put her through a basic obedience course, which will teach her to respect the leash, respect your wishes, and give her some quality time with you.

Make sure your dog can reach the back door from her tether. This will help her feel less abandoned. Make sure there are a couple of swivels in the line to keep it from getting twisted and double-check that there is nothing she can tangle herself in, especially around the back door.

When you need to leave your dog outside, make sure she has a cozy doghouse, shade, toys to play with and gnaw on, a sandbox to dig in, water to drink, and a wading pool in the summer. Make her area fun and entertaining and she will be less bored and upset.

WARNING: Never tie your dog where she can leap off of something and hang herself, such as the bed of a pickup truck, the edge of a deck or stairs, or the bank of a steep ravine. Never tie your dog on a choke chain, which may tangle and choke her. Also never tie your dog up for a long period or in unfamiliar areas; she could get stolen or tormented.

URINATING AND DEFECATING IN THE DOG BED

Problem: When I confine my dog to his crate, he relieves himself in it.

Why your dog is doing this: Dogs don't normally mess their sleeping area. Your dog may have been confined for too long a period before he had complete control of his bladder and bowels. If the crate was too big, he may have been able to curl up in one end and relieve himself in the other. Or he may not have been allowed to relieve himself before he was crated.

What to say and do:

1. Make sure the crate is not too big. It should be just large enough for your dog to stretch out and stand up straight in. If it is too big, block off the back end by stuffing it securely with a cardboard box.

2. Put the crate in an accessible area—the family room, for example—and securely prop open the door. Put treats in the crate. Encourage your dog to take naps in his crate by making it the only bed available for him to use. Don't shut him in it, though. When he has been using the crate for naps for a couple of weeks, you can begin confining him for brief periods, but make sure he relieves himself beforehand.

3. If he still messes the crate, take the lid off and let him use just the bottom half. If your crate does not come in two halves, use a large cardboard box with no top on it. Set this up on a slightly raised surface, so he can jump or walk up to it. If the crate is in a pen, put papers on the floor all around it.

4. Take out any excess bedding and give him a flat piece of rug, so he can't get away from or bury his mess. If that doesn't work, take the crate away for a while, and give him just the rug on the raised platform, then slowly work your way back to the covered crate.

5. When you must leave him alone, provide him with access to a potty area near his crate or sleeping area. If you want to housebreak him to go outside and you have a dog door, put the crate next to the dog door so your dog can sleep in the crate and relieve himself outdoors. If you don't have a dog door, put papers down for him next to his crate in his confined area.

Why this works: Dogs do not like to mess where they sleep. Stopping all confinement in the crate and giving your dog continual access to a convenient potty area will give him somewhere to go other than his bed. By elevating his sleeping area, you give him a ledge or perch from which he can view his domain; this gives him an even more obvious separation between bed and papers. Once your dog has an alternative to messing the crate, he will do his best to avoid doing so when you begin to confine him again.

Prevention: Don't confine your dog to the crate without getting him used to it gradually. Make sure the crate isn't too big, or he will be able to relieve himself in one end and sleep in the other.

Have your vet check your dog for any infections, especially urinary. Some medications upset a dog's stomach or make him very thirsty so he drinks and piddles more. Always let your dog relieve himself before you put him in the crate; it is cruel not to do so.

See also:
Crate training

URINATING, INVOLUNTARY

Problem: Whenever I come home or someone else comes over, my dog piddles when he is petted.

Why your dog is doing this: Your dog is overjoyed and excited to see humans. He is also slightly nervous and submissive by nature. This combination leads to involuntary urinating.

What to say and do:

1. When you first come in the door, ignore your dog entirely for three or four minutes until he has stopped wiggling around wildly and wondering why you won't pet him.

2. Then squat down, say hello, keep your hands slow and low, pet him under the chin and on the chest, and take him outside immediately to urinate. If he starts to piddle in the house, don't reprimand him—it will only make him urinate more. Stop petting him and ignore him until he calms down.

3. Instruct all visitors to ignore your dog until he settles down. Have them pet him with slow hands.

Why this works: When your dog is overexcited at greeting you, the added stimulus of being petted is more than he can handle. Waiting a few minutes until he settles down will help him control his bladder.

Prevention: It is in your dog's basic nature to be submissive, and he shows his submission by urinating. All you can do is tone down the greetings. If your dog knows how to do a sit-stay, try that. By instructing him to hold a position, you are asking him to exercise some self-control, which may in turn help him control his urinating. Put him in a sit-stay before you pet him, and be sure to use slow hands, since fast or playful handling will lead to more piddling. Putting your dog through an upbeat, positive obedience program will build his confidence. And don't fret: most dogs eventually grow out of this habit.

See also:
Abused
Shyness

Urinating to Mark Territory

Problem: My dog keeps lifting his leg in the house and urinating on everything. He used to do this only occasionally, but now that we have another dog he does it all the time.

Why your dog is doing this: Leg lifting is how dogs mark their territory. Your dog is reminding everyone in the house, including the new dog, that he runs the show.

What to say and do:

1. Enroll your dog in an obedience program, and practice the commands in the house. Do lots of down-stays next to the areas and objects he has been marking.

2. Put him on a strict housebreaking program. Crate training is an essential component in this program, since the confinement keeps him from marking his territory in the house.

3. Get your intact male neutered. Until the urge to reproduce is removed, most dogs who have gotten into the habit of marking in the house won't stop until they are neutered.

4. If you catch him marking, get him in a scruff grip and reprimand him very firmly: "No! Bad!" Take him outside or confine him in his crate while you clean up after him.

5. If you don't catch him in the act, don't bother to correct him—it won't do any good—but keep a close eye on him. Chances are if he's hanging out in the area he marked, he'll casually glance at or sniff the spot. If he does, growl at him and shoo him away. He will eventually return to the same marking spots to freshen them up, so be on the lookout and ambush him.

6. Do not leave him unattended in the house until he is thoroughly housebroken.

Why this works: Having your male dog neutered, giving him formal obedience training, and putting him on a housebreaking program using a crate will increase your chances of successfully solving this problem. If you leave out even one of those steps your chances drop considerably. The obedience training elevates you to pack-leader status; the housebreaking routine limits his access indoors, puts him on a schedule, and gets him in the habit of peeing outside; and neutering helps control his hormones.

Prevention: Neutering, housebreaking, and early obedience training usually prevent this problem from occurring.

See also:
Crate training
Heat, male

URINATING WHEN REPRIMANDED

Problem: My dog pees whenever I raise my voice or try to make her do something she doesn't want to do, such as get off the furniture.

Why your dog is doing this: Your dog is frightened, and fearful urinating is classic submissive behavior for a dog. Perhaps your corrections are too harsh for her temperament.

What to say and do:

1. Make the punishment fit the crime. If your dog is mildly out of line, you don't need to bellow at her to get her attention. Tone down your corrections, and instruct other household members to do the same. Praise your dog as soon as she responds correctly.

2. Many dogs urinate submissively when they are corrected by men, since men are big and have deep voices. Make sure the time your dog spends with men is warm and nonthreatening.

3. Practice obedience training with lots of caring, praise, and love so that your dog will learn to respect you as the compassionate leader of the pack. This training will also make her feel safe and give her confidence, so her tendency to pee out of fear will be diminished.

4. If anyone has been teasing your dog, put a stop to it at once.

Why this works: Keeping your voice down will let your dog know that submissive urinating is not necessary. Obedience training will give her confidence in herself and in you, so that her fear will diminish and the submissive urination will gradually cease.

Prevention: Basic obedience training will build confidence in an insecure dog. It is especially important for any men in the house to practice the training with the dog, if she is reacting most fearfully to them. This will also help men view their dog without the anger, frustration, and disgust that often accompany the experience of having their dog pee every time she's corrected.

Find a quiet place and spend twenty minutes a day giving your dog a calming massage. This will help her relax, learn to trust you, and enjoy your touch. It is especially important that anyone she is afraid of do the massage work on her as well. Be sure to talk to her soothingly during the massage so she will associate a calming voice with your calm hands. Then, when she's frightened of something or needlessly worried, you can soothe her with your voice and hands.

If your dog is unusually sensitive, get professional help to ensure that she is taught in the kindest possible manner and one that is tailored to her particular needs.

Never let anyone tease or yell at your dog.

See also:
Abused dog
Hand-shyness
Nervousness
Shyness

VETERINARIAN, FEAR OF

Problem: My dog gets scared when we go to the vet. I have to drag her through the door. Then she sits there trembling or tries to escape.

Why your dog is doing this: If your dog has had a painful or unpleasant experience—often unavoidable—at the vet's office, she will be afraid to return. Getting poked by needles and thermometers doesn't make for pleasant memories, nor does being handled by strangers in a foreign and strange-smelling environment.

What to say and do:

1. Teach your dog some simple obedience commands at home and practice them until she knows them well. This will give you a way to control her when she's frightened and will build up her confidence.

2. Spend twenty minutes every day giving her a calming massage, and then incorporate it into her training sessions so that you'll be able to help her settle down when you take her to the vet.

3. When she's learned some commands and relaxes easily under your hands, take her to the veterinary clinic on a training-and-socializing visit. First, practice her obedience commands in front of the clinic, incorporating some massage on her sits. When she relaxes and is paying attention to you, heel her in and out of the door, talking happily to her. Continue her obedience commands and calming massage in the waiting area.

4. Have the staff give her some special yummy treats you provide, like liver bits or cheese. When she's relaxed in the waiting area, ask if you can walk her through the hallways and examining rooms. Allow her to sniff around and stop to do some massage, feed her treats, or practice some easy sit-stays. Praise her lavishly for responding.

5. Once she seems comfortable, place her gently on an examining table. (If she's a big dog, you may need help.) Once she's on the table, give her a massage, feed her some treats and have the staff do so too. Practice having her up on an elevated surface at home (a washer or dryer works for small dogs).

6. If possible, have the veterinarian and some of the staff sit on the floor of the exam room or the waiting area with you. Let her check everyone out, especially the vet, and have everyone feed her treats and scratch her in her favorite places.

7. Make as many of these training trips as necessary. If possible, don't schedule any treatment for her until she is relaxed and under control at the clinic.

Why this works: Giving your dog a chance to familiarize herself with the clinic and staff when nothing unpleasant is going to be done helps her form a positive association with the place. The obedience work gives her confidence, and the calming work, now done in the clinic, helps her to relax.

Prevention: If you provide socialization, grooming, bathing, and obedience training, your dog isn't likely to be fearful of the vet. A puppy who has had frequent, pleasant handling and restraint training will be a tolerant patient, even when being treated for an injury. Pick your veterinarian not only for his or her medical expertise, but for a compassionate and respectful bedside manner toward both you and your dog. Crate-training your dog will help her feel comfortable at the vet's when she needs to stay for treatment.

See also:
Crate training

WILD BEHAVIOR IN THE HOUSE

Problem: Whenever I let my dog in the house, he is so wild that I have to put him back outside almost immediately.

Why your dog is doing this: When dogs spend all their time alone and outside, they can be desperate for company, so when they come inside and are with their humans they are beside themselves with joy and consequently bounce off the walls.

What to say and do:

1. Teach your dog some obedience commands, especially sit and stay. Make sure he understands how to control himself on a leash. Practice his training outside at first, where he spends most of his time.

2. Spend a minimum of twenty minutes a day outside with your dog, giving him a calming massage. If necessary, use the leash to control him and have him maintain a sit-stay. It may take some time to build him up to a twenty-minute massage; so spend twenty minutes or so in obedience practice to settle him.

3. If he is still too wild for the obedience training and massage, spend a half hour playing with him in the yard beforehand. After several days of this routine, bring him inside on-leash. Practice the obedience exercises in the house, limiting him to a couple of rooms. When he settles down, find a quiet spot and give him a long massage. When he is relaxed, take the leash off and let him sniff around.

4. Give him a cozy bed inside the house, as well as some indoor toys he can focus on. Don't let him have the run of the house; continue to limit him to a couple of rooms. Introduce him to the rest of the house in the same way—first on-leash with training and massage, then off-leash. Provide toys wherever he is hanging out.

5. He may zoom around for a bit when you first let him off the leash, but he will probably settle down after the initial excitement has passed.

6. If you can't trust him loose in the house when you are not watching him, crate-train him so that he can stay inside when you can't monitor him. When he is crate-trained, have him sleep in his crate next to your bed at night. That will settle him down considerably and make him very happy.

Why this works: Your dog must be given enough time indoors to get over his initial excitement at being inside with you. Preparing him for his entry by teaching him a few obedience commands and doing some calming massage gives you a chance to learn how to work and relax together, so that when you bring him inside, the routine will have already been established.

Prevention: Banishing your dog to a life of solitary confinement in the yard is as cruel as it is common in this country. Dogs are pack animals, and as such they crave company; as loving beings they are capable of forming deep, lasting bonds. Banishment leads to intense loneliness and can contribute to a variety of problems, one of which is wildness upon finally coming into contact with other living creatures (including you!).

Socializing your dog to the house at a young age prevents the house and its residents from becoming so special that your dog goes bananas when he is allowed to come in. Include your dog in your daily life. Take him for walks in the neighborhood or for rides in the car and find him a doggy playmate if he likes other dogs. If you can afford it, puppy kindergarten or obedience classes will give you something useful and fun to do with your dog and will help create a strong bond. Remember, dogs weren't meant to pine away alone in the yard—so don't let them.

See also:
Crate training
Excitable behavior
Hyperactivity
Zooming

ZOOMING

Problem: Every so often my dog will zoom around the house as though he were on a racecourse. There's no stopping him!

Why your dog is doing this: Your dog is letting off excess energy, which has built up as a result of not getting enough exercise. This is especially true for house or apartment dogs who have no yard to run in and are always exercised on a leash.

What to say and do:

1. This is the time to whoop it up and have a blast with your dog. Clap your hands and join him in the festivities. As he comes careening past you, grab playfully at his rump, encouraging him to run more. Jump up and down on the couch and yelp away happily.

2. Chase your dog around the house and then hide behind a door and goose him as he flies by. Make silly hissing noises. Crawl around on all fours, barking, howling, and slapping the floor with excitement. Your dog will look forward to these moments more eagerly than you ever could imagine.

Why this works: Joining your dog in his joyful moments is fun for everyone—a time to be wild and silly yourself. It's a grand way to let him know you love him and appreciate his goofy, carefree nature. When you participate in his fun, you let him see that you are lighthearted and silly too. These precious moments help you and your dog bond in the joy of being alive.

Prevention: If you don't want your dog to cut loose in the house, make sure he gets plenty of outdoor exercise—running, jumping, romping, and playing with other friendly dogs. Otherwise your dog will have to let off steam and stay healthy by zooming around the house.

Be aware that no matter how much exercise he gets, you should be prepared for a wild zooming session after a bath! (It's probably the way we feel after a great swim in the ocean—refreshed, cleansed, and ready to party.)

See also:

Wild behavior in the house

INDEX